= gold ribbon

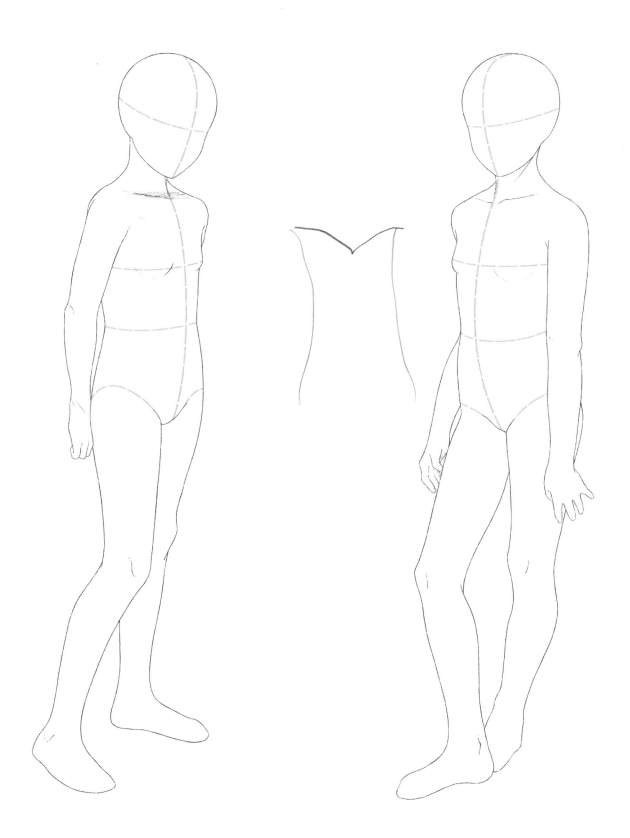

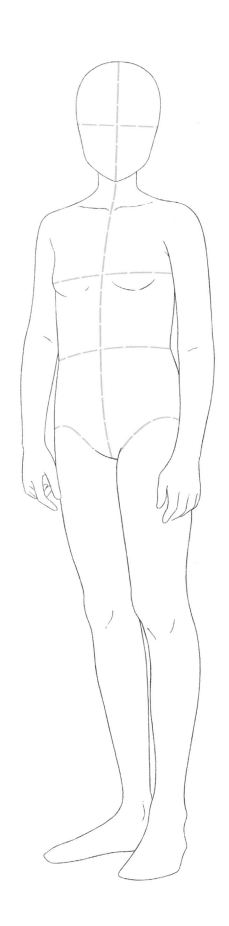
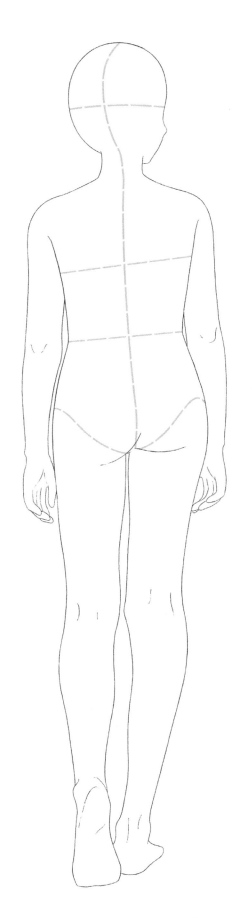

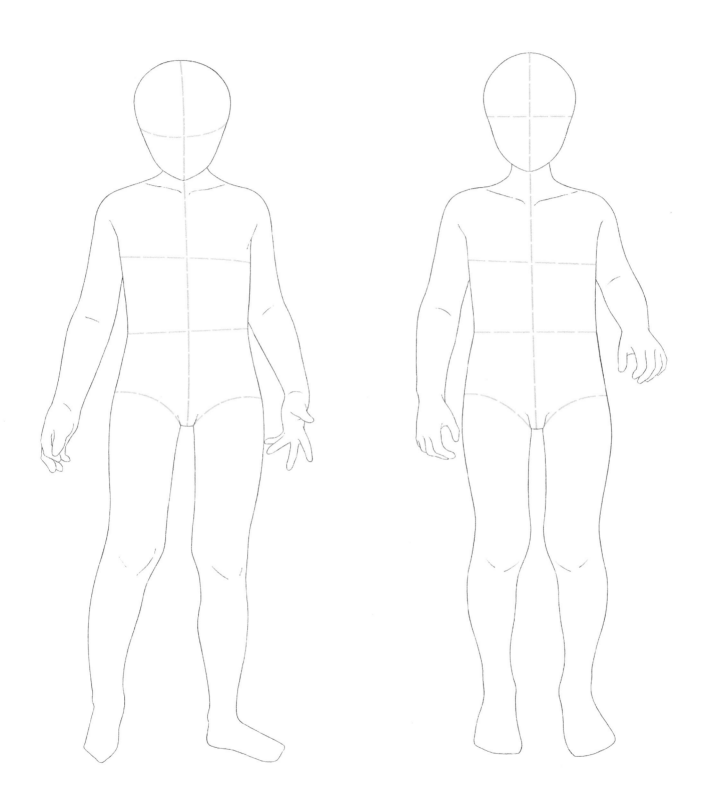

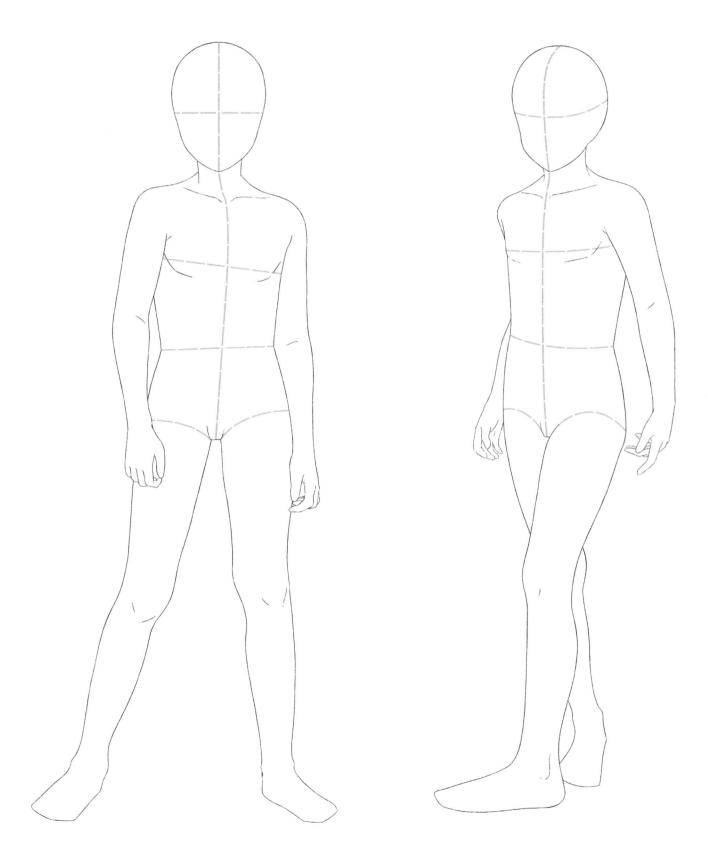

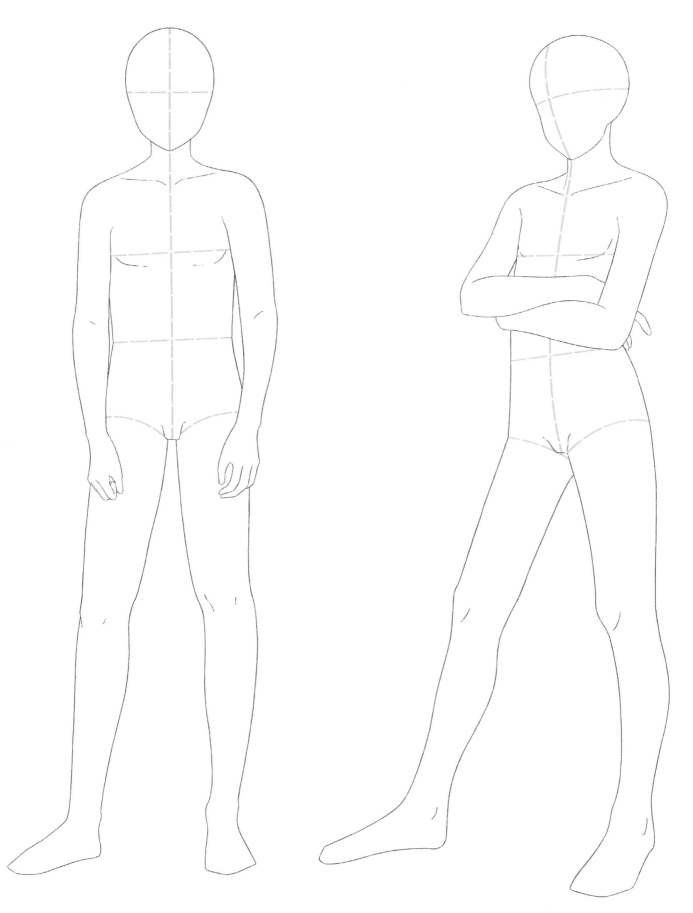

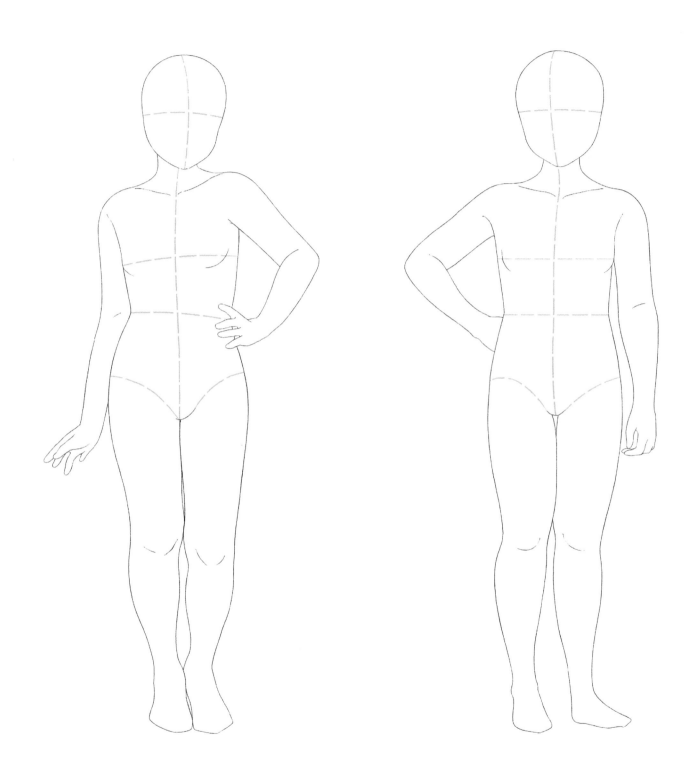

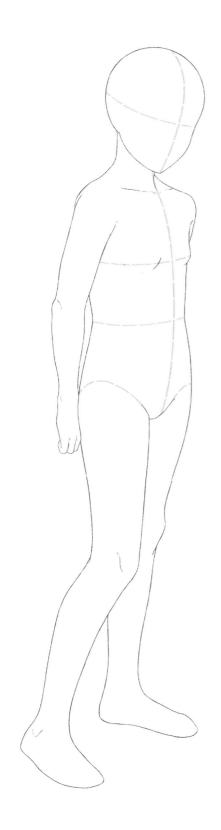
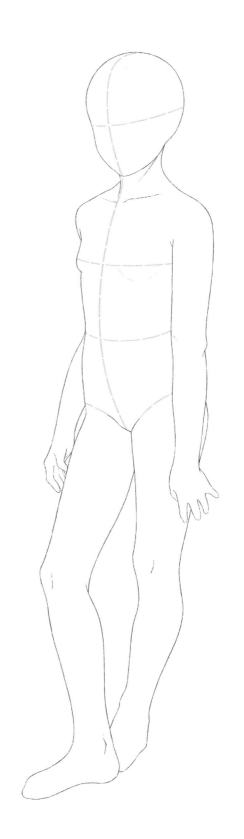

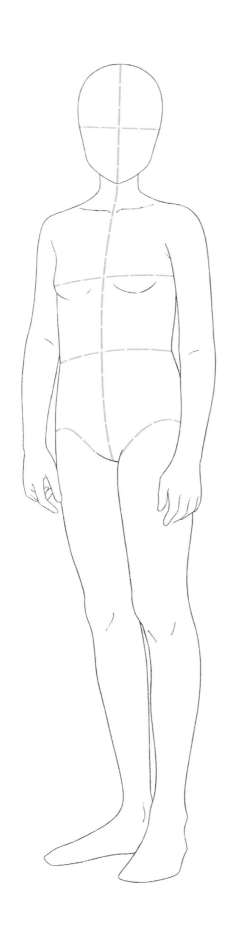
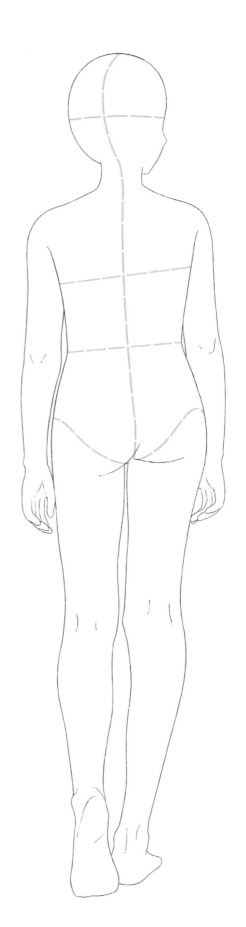

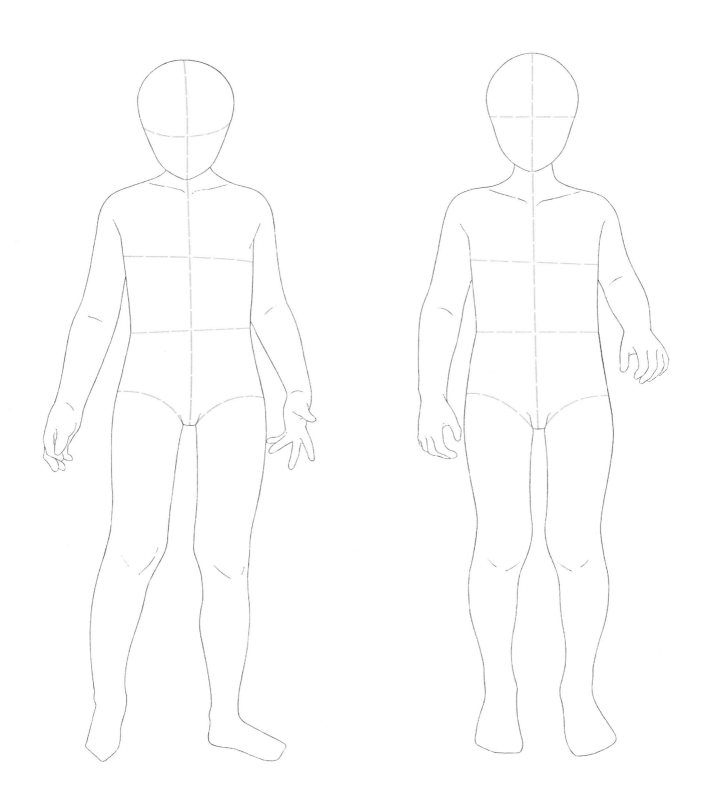

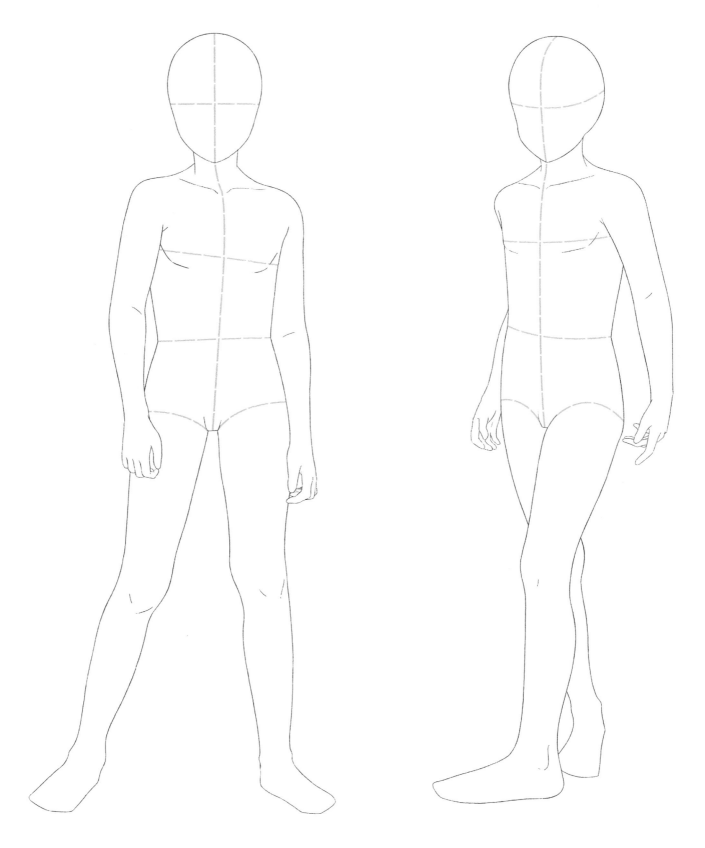

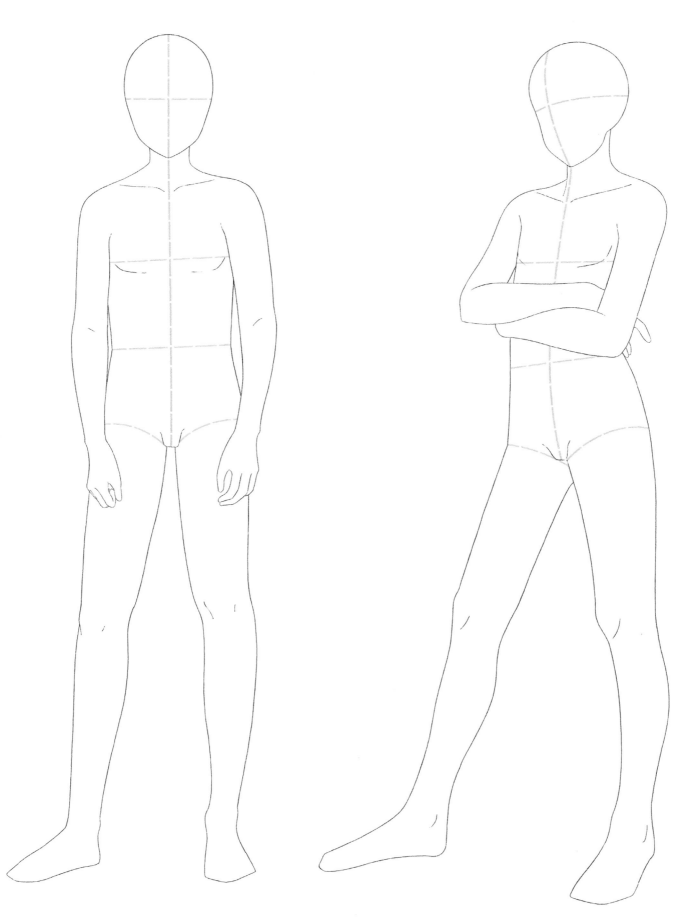

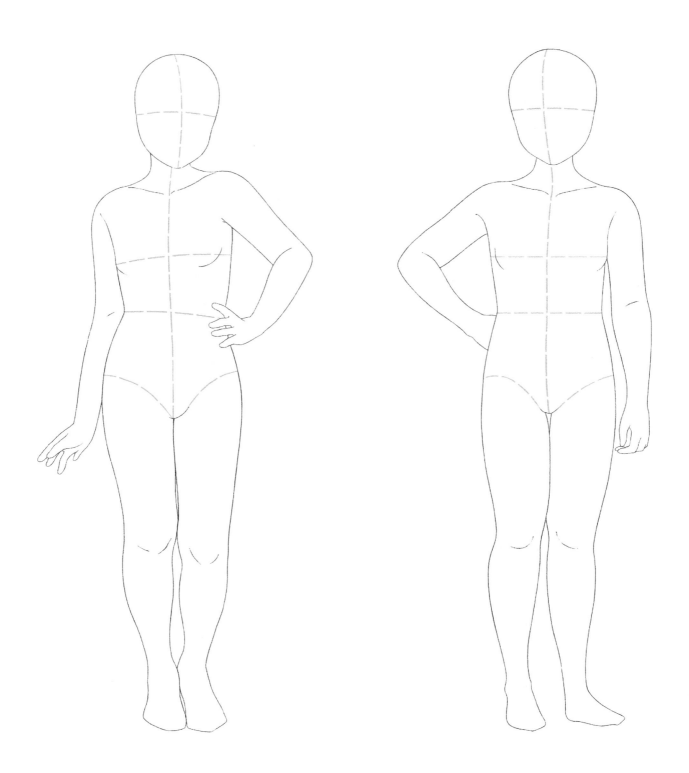

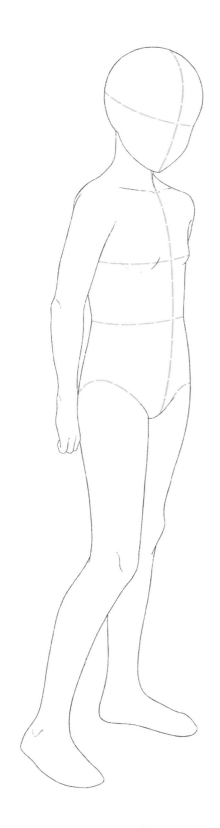
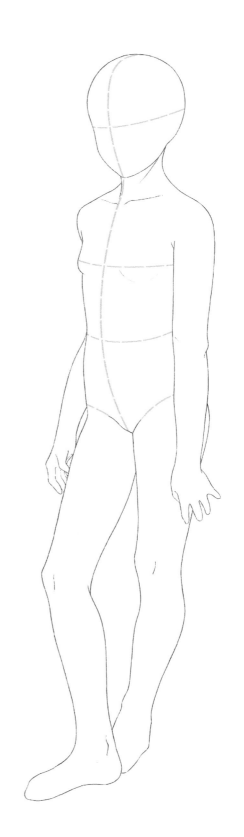

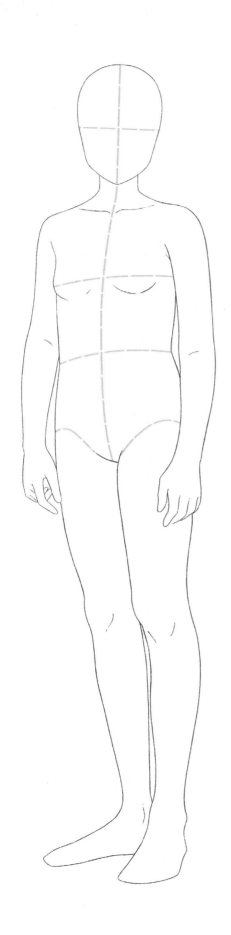
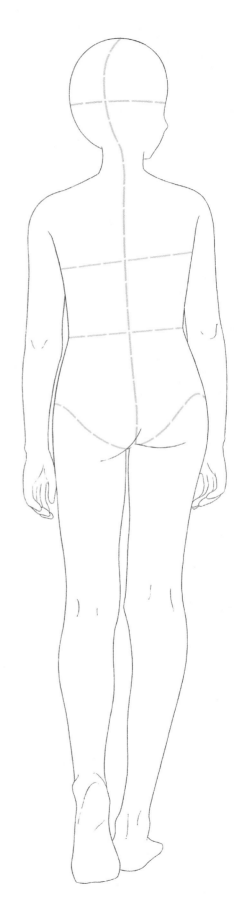

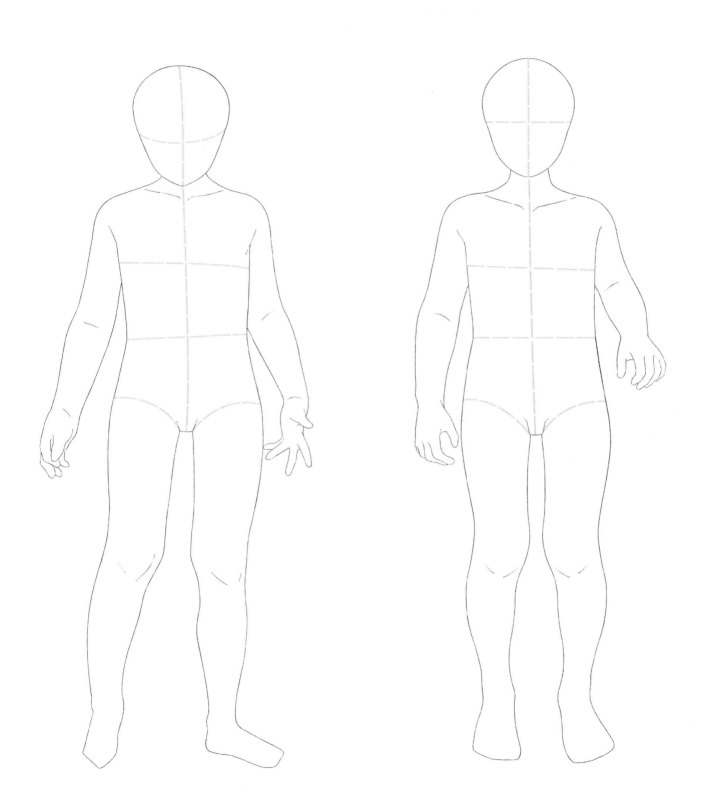

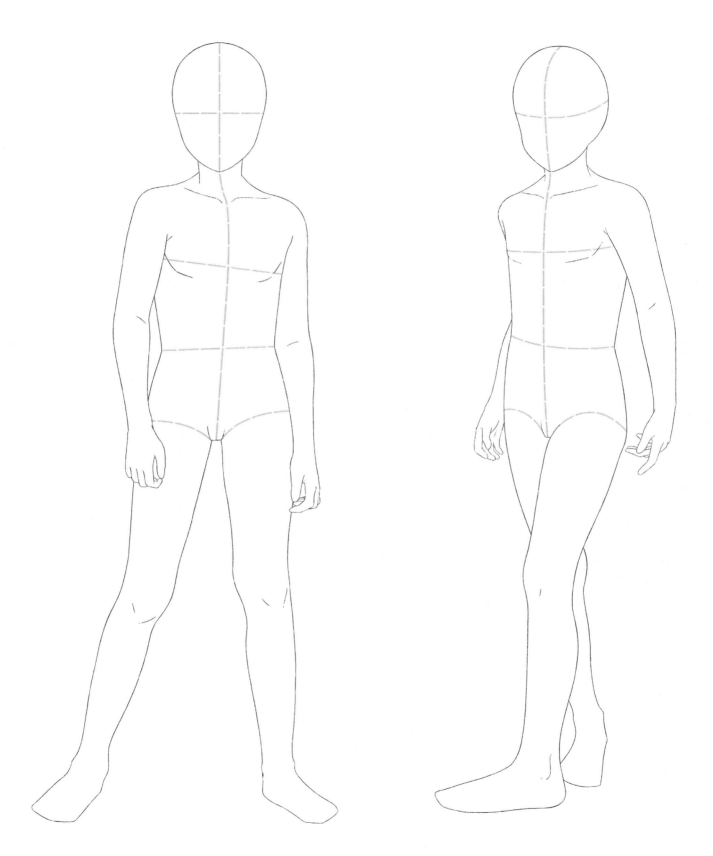

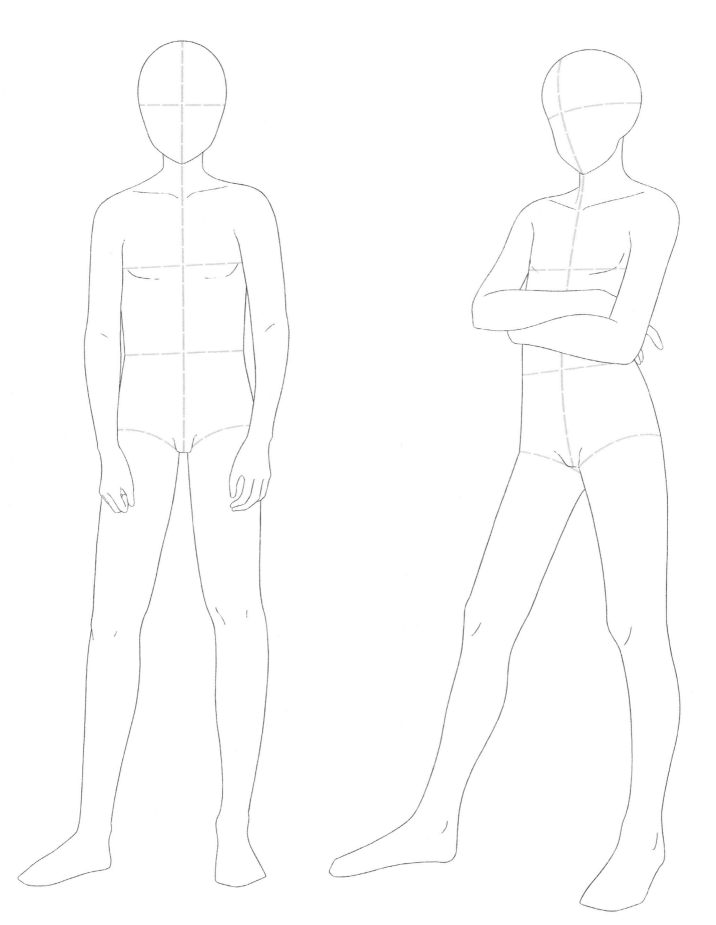

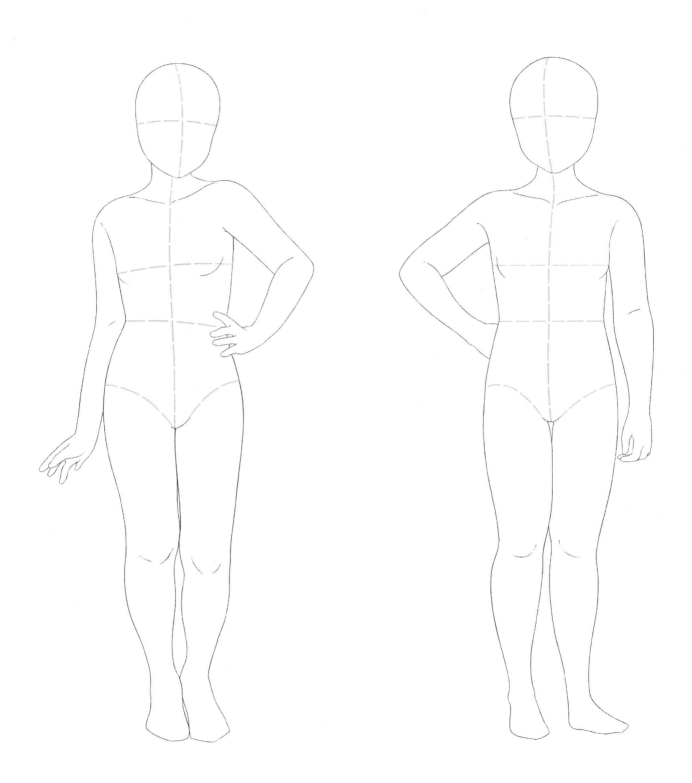

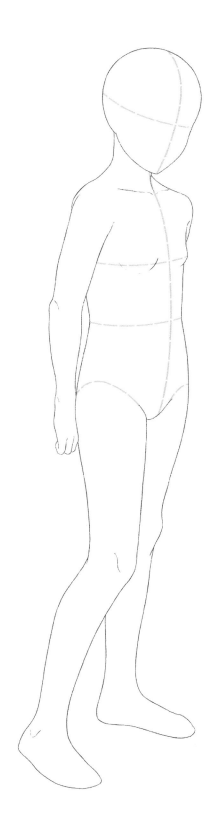
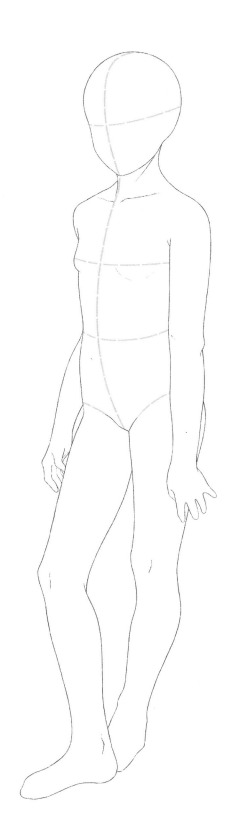

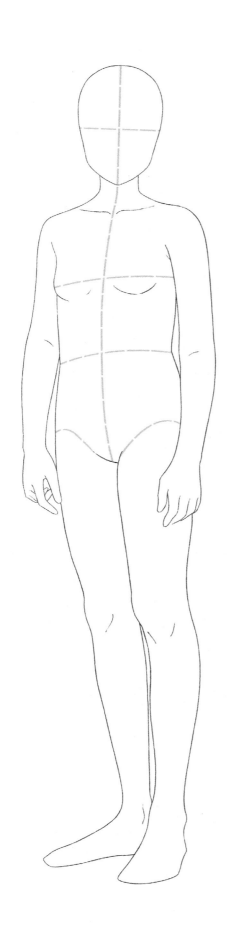
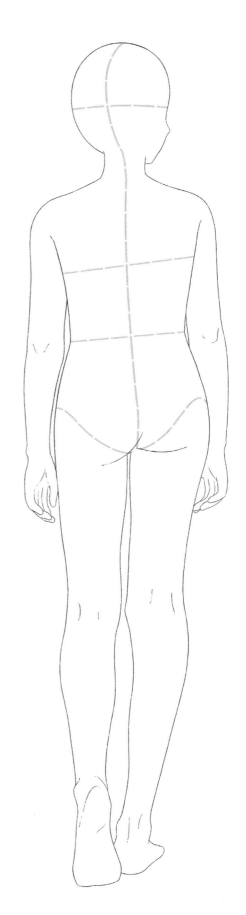

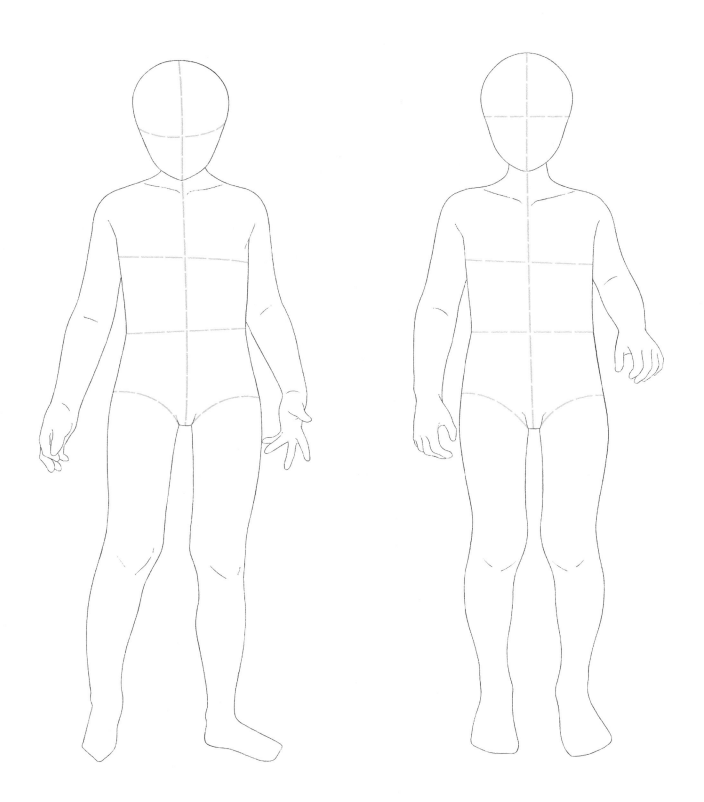

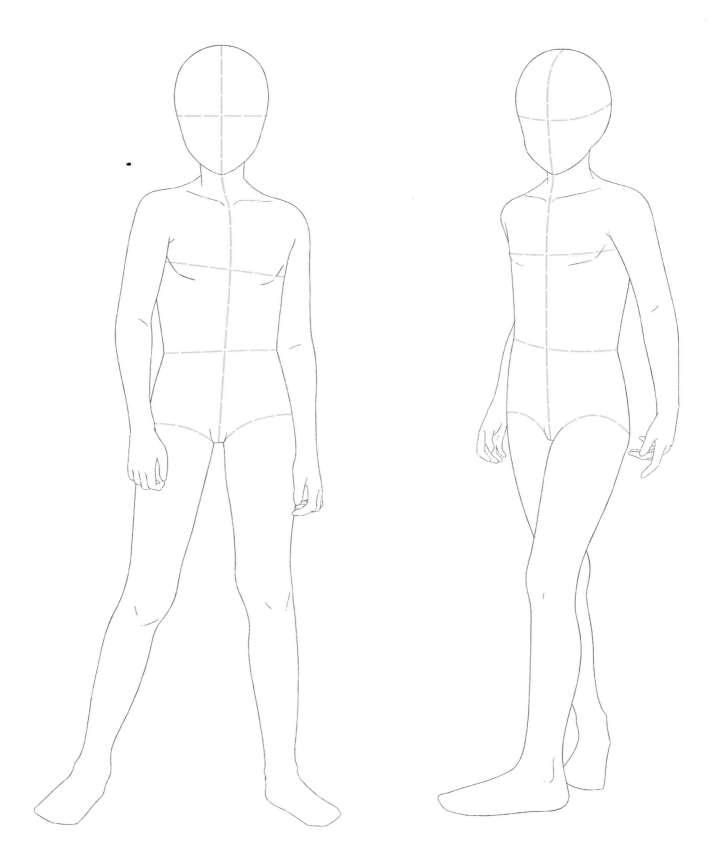

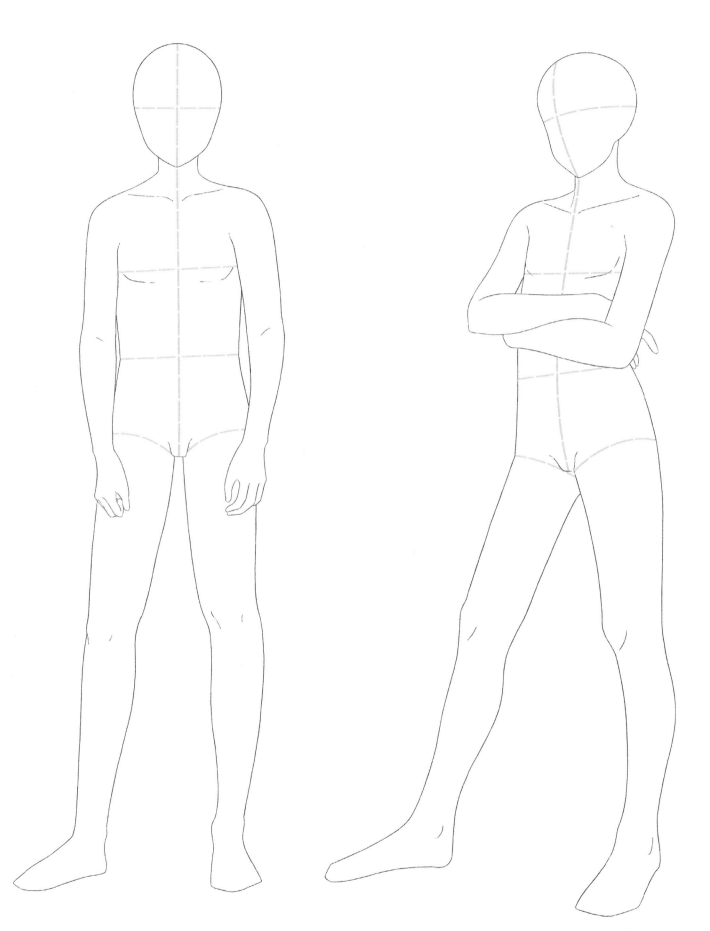

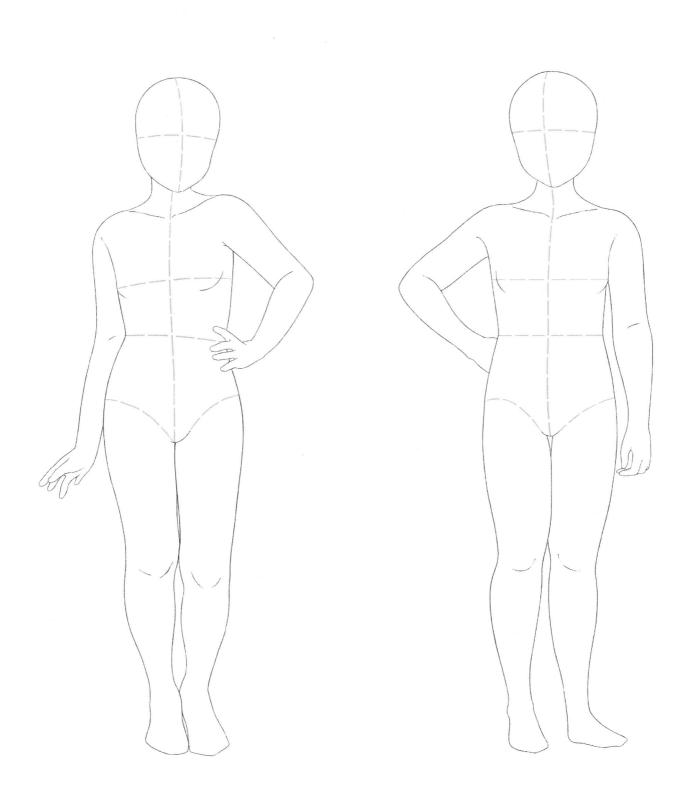

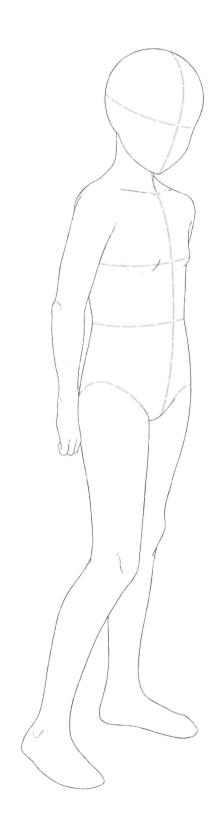
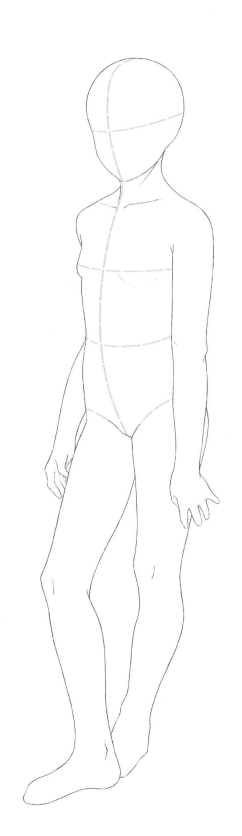

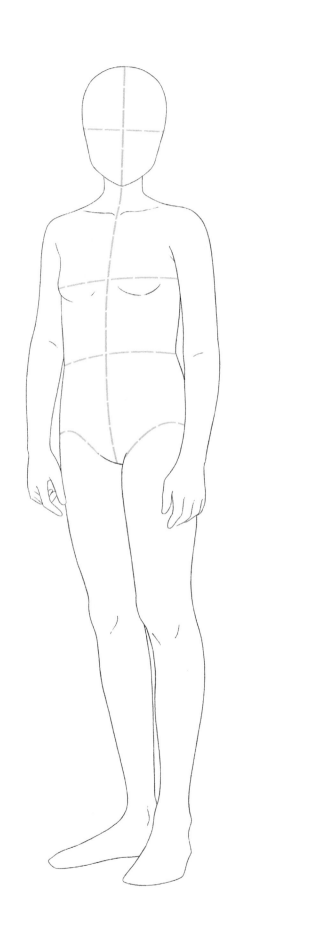
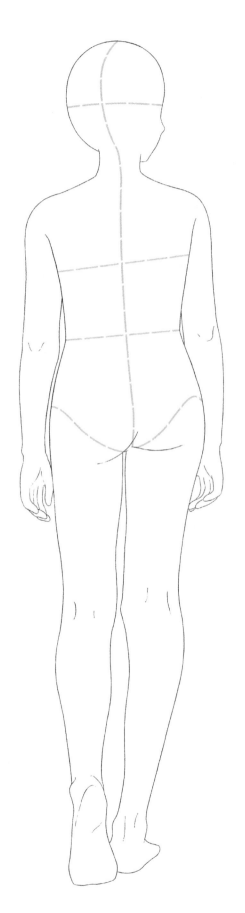

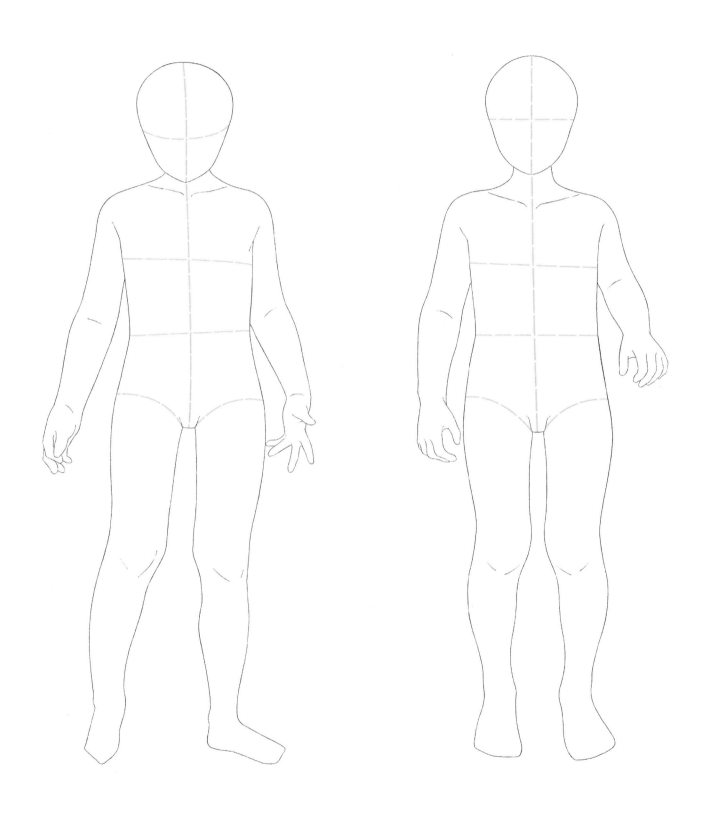

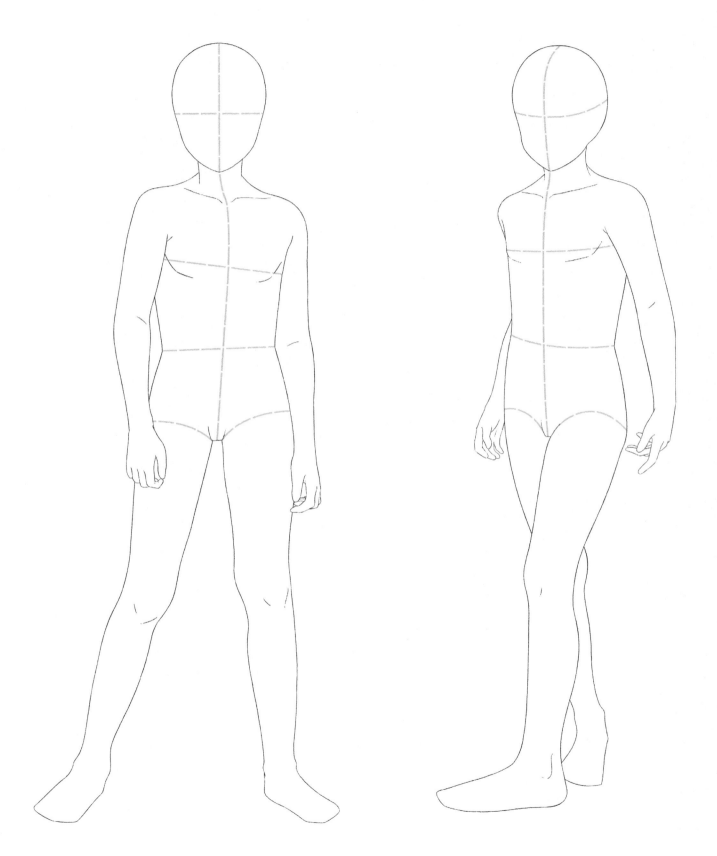

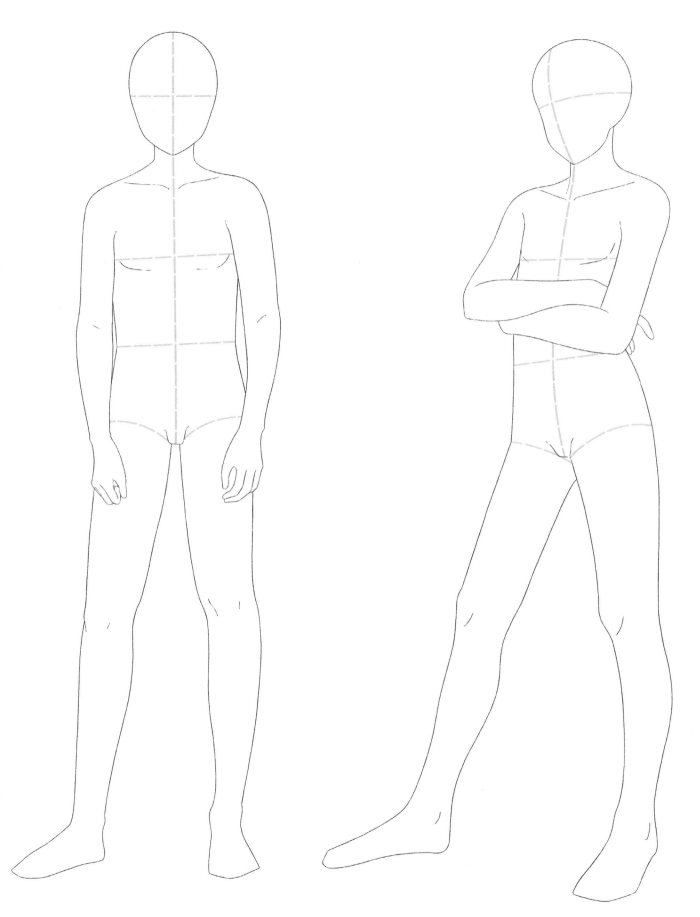

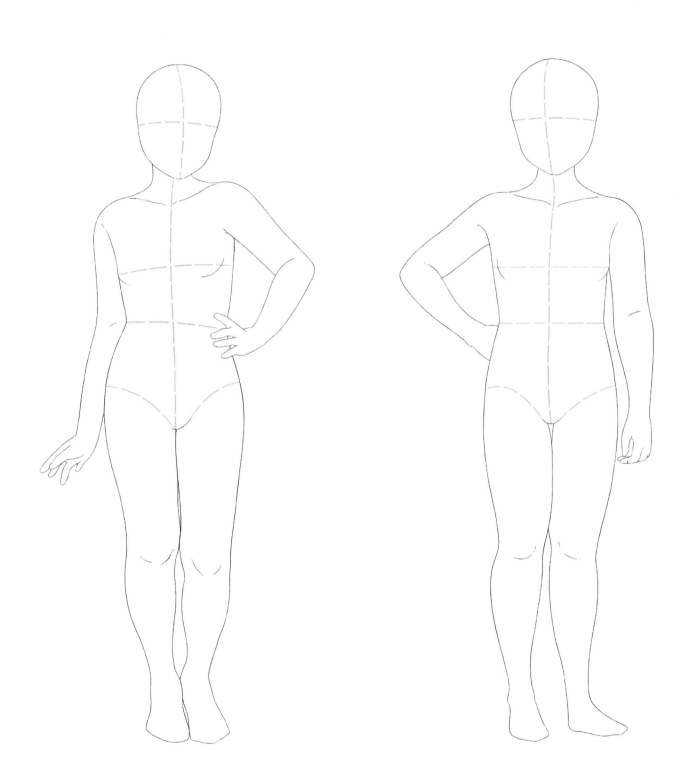

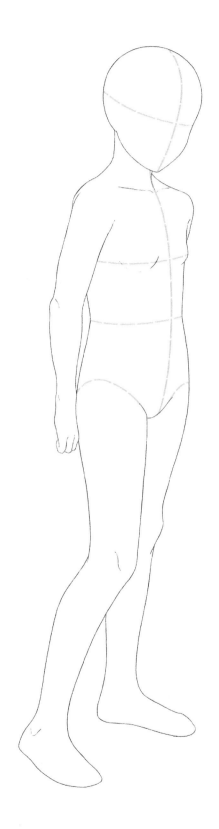
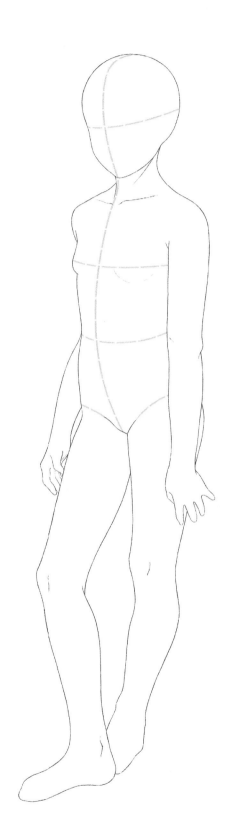

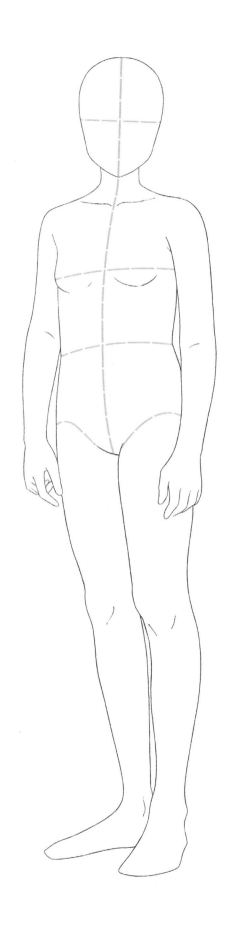
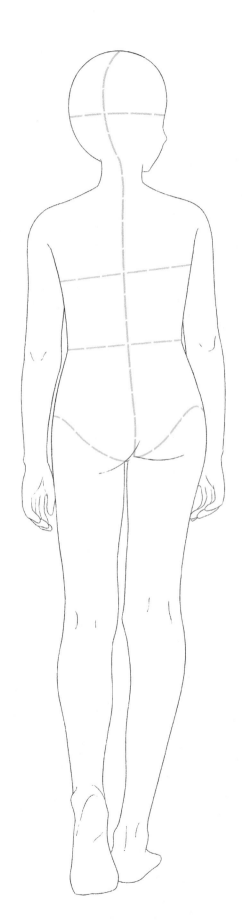

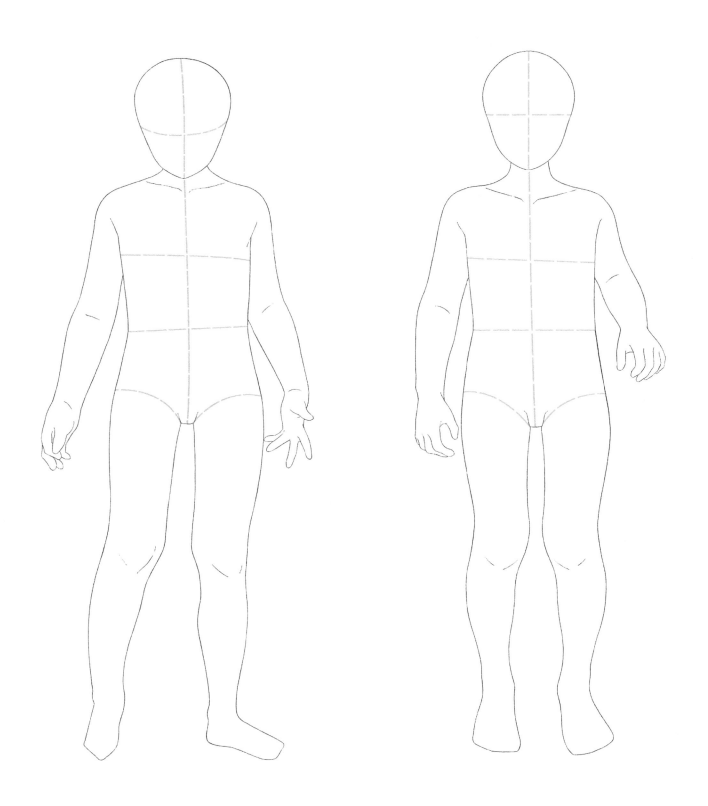

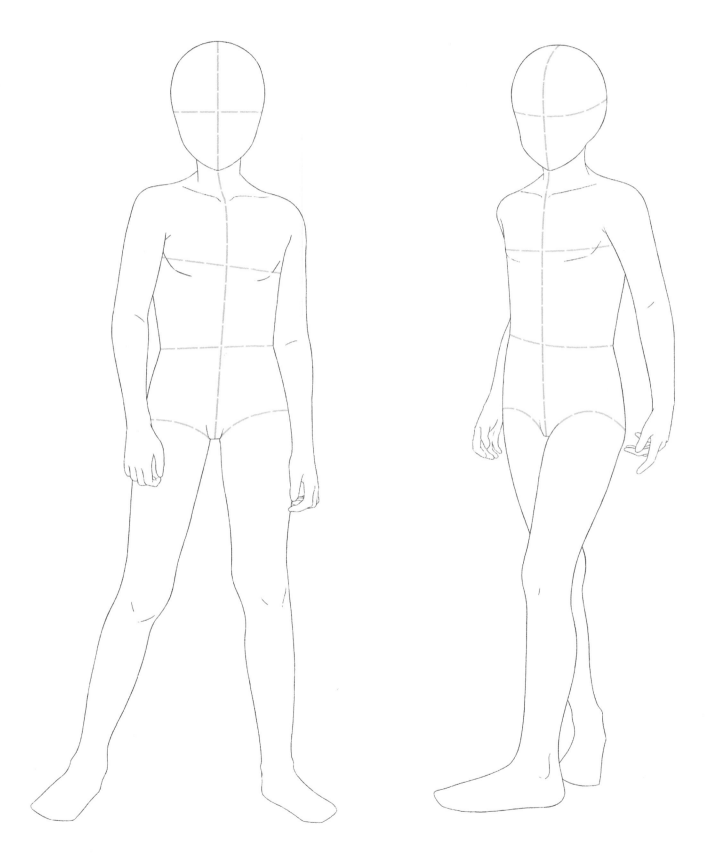

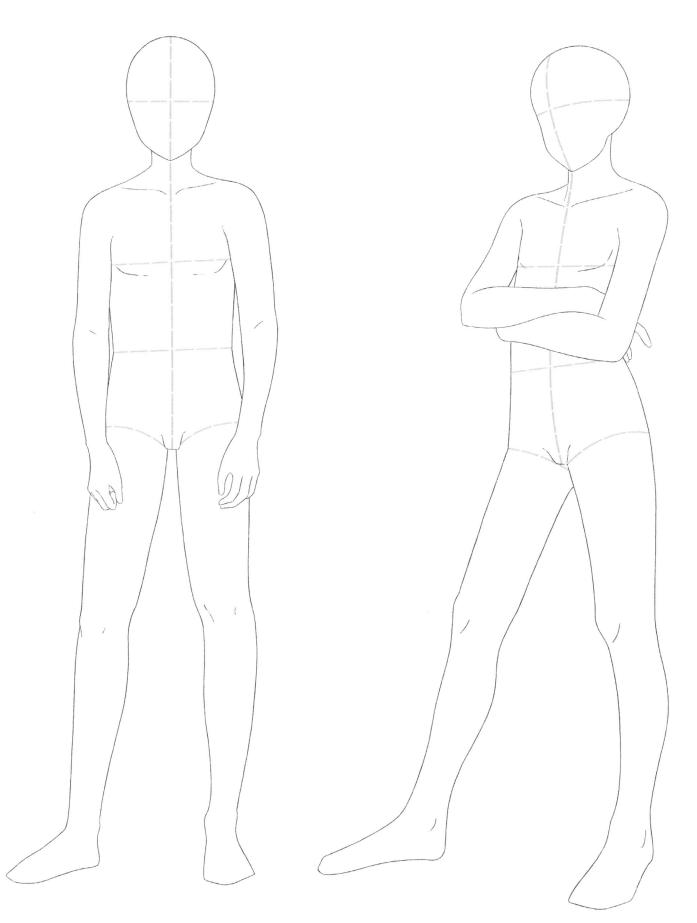

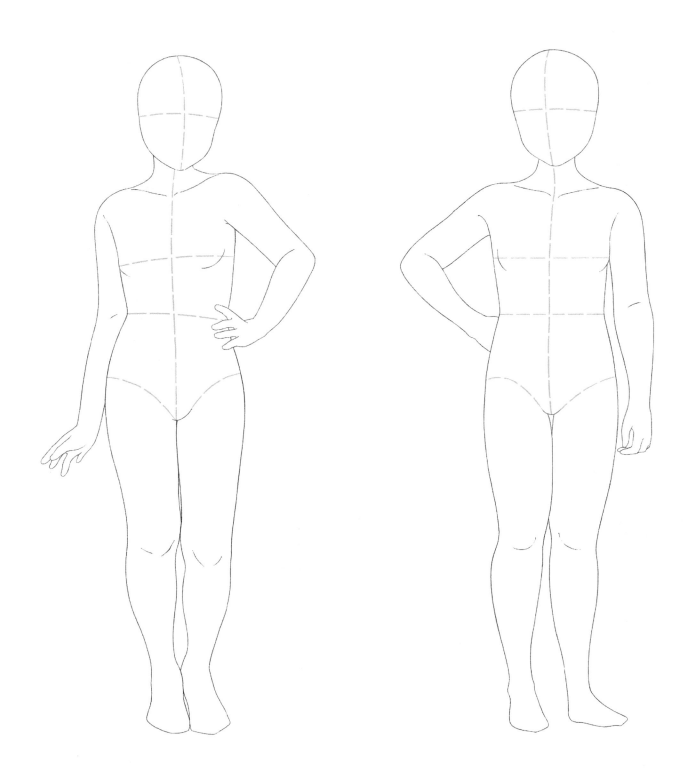

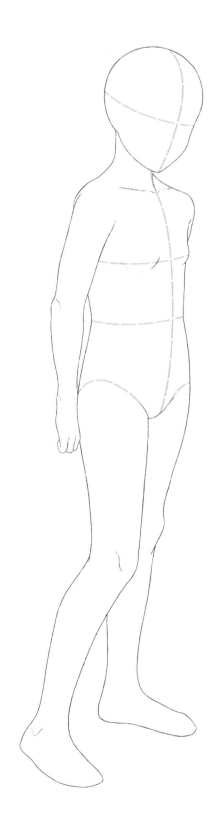
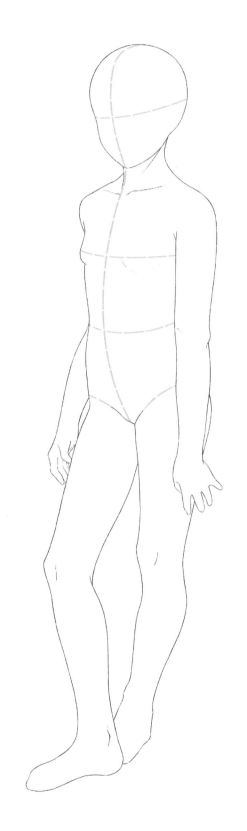

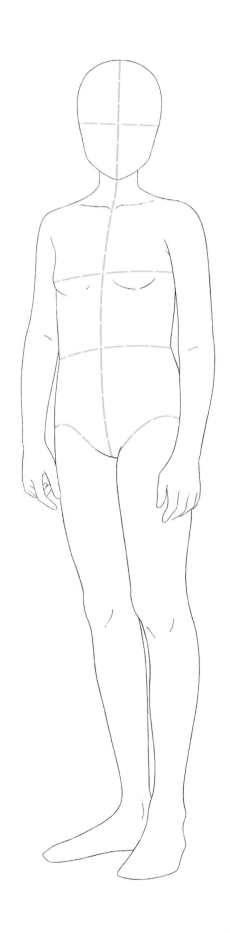
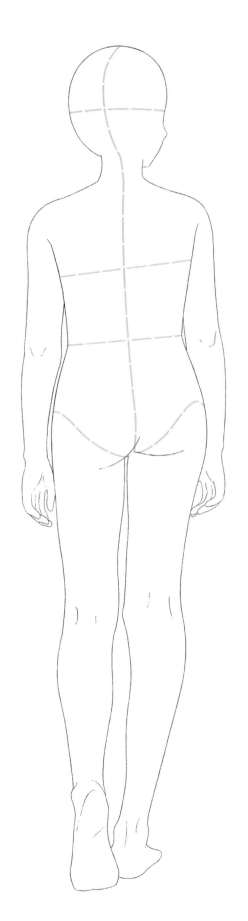

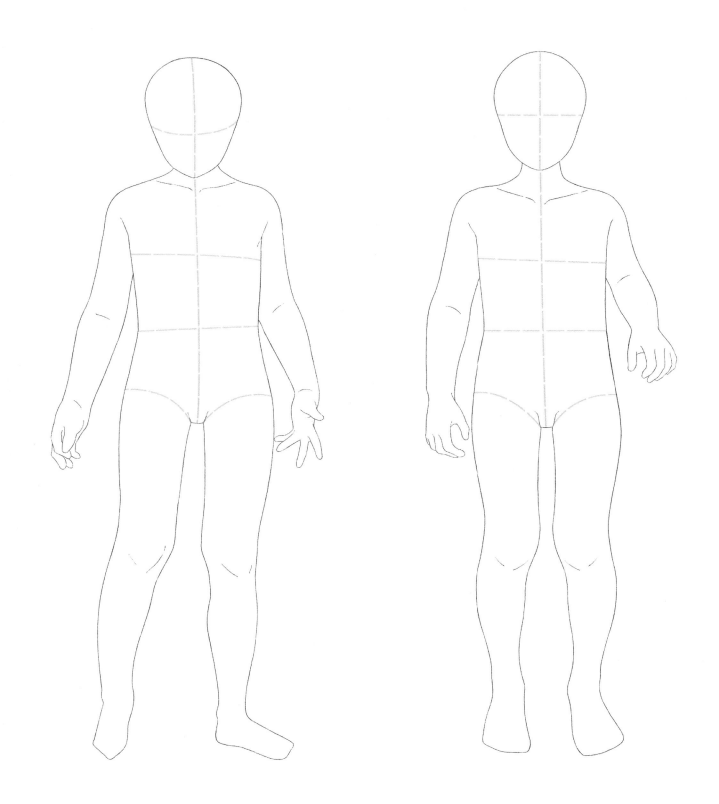

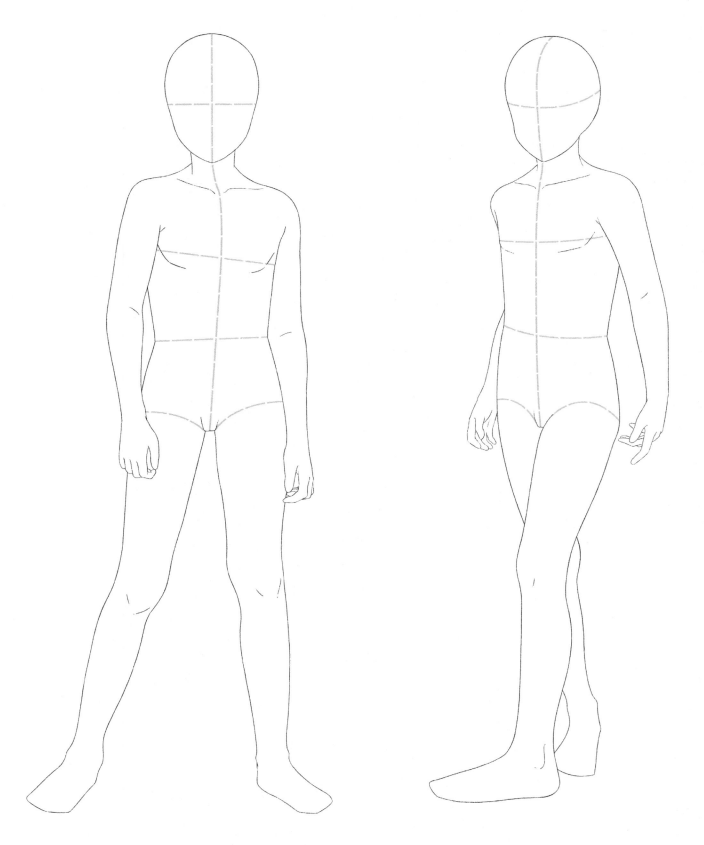

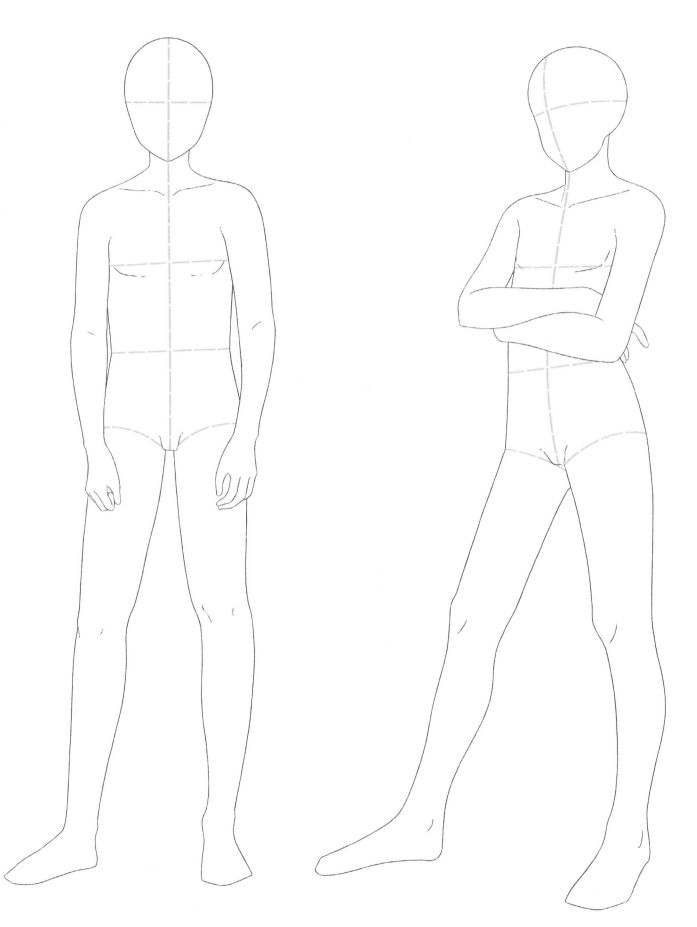

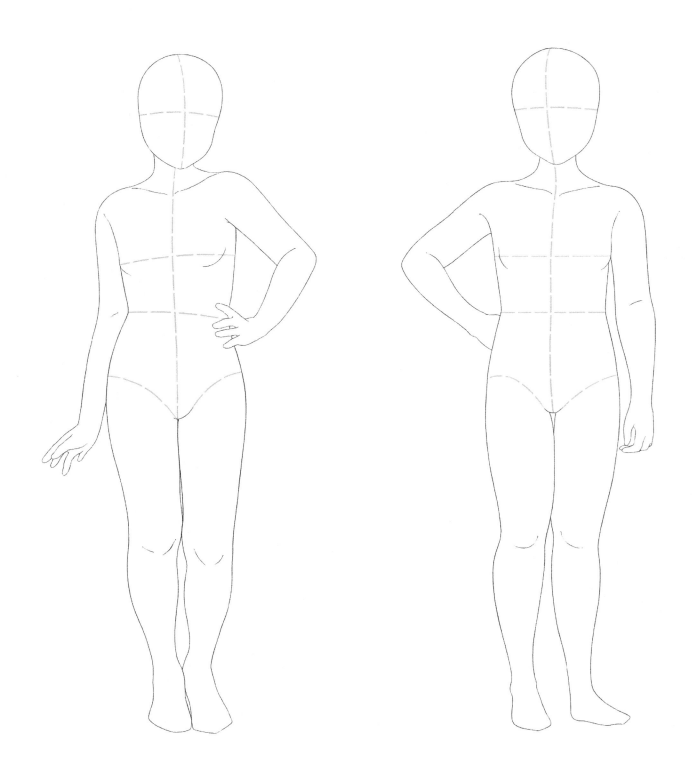

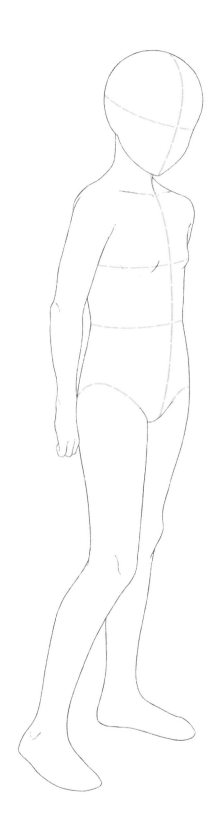
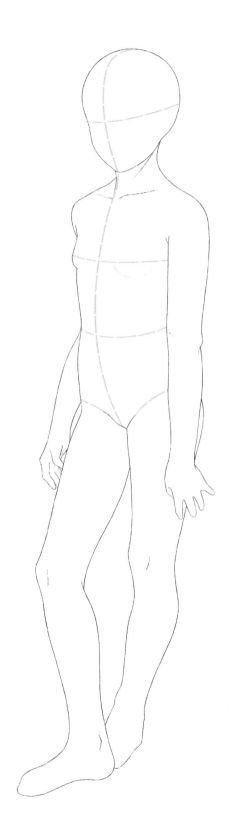

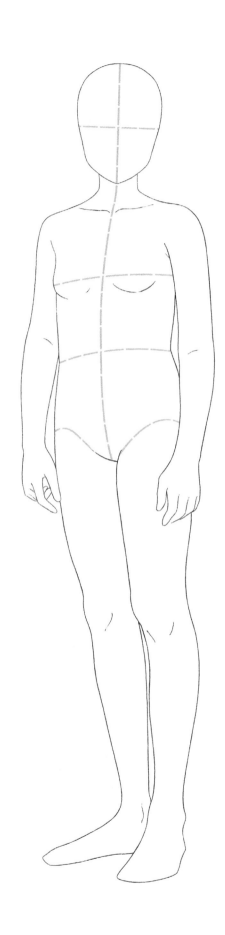
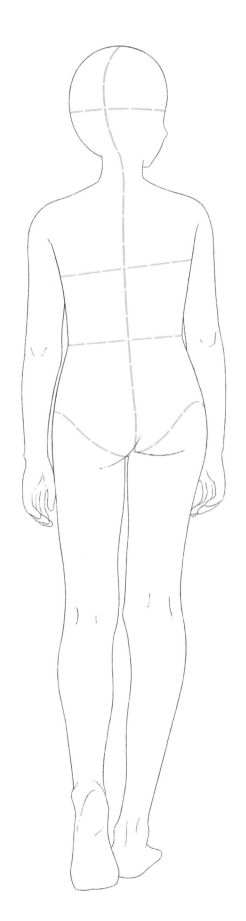

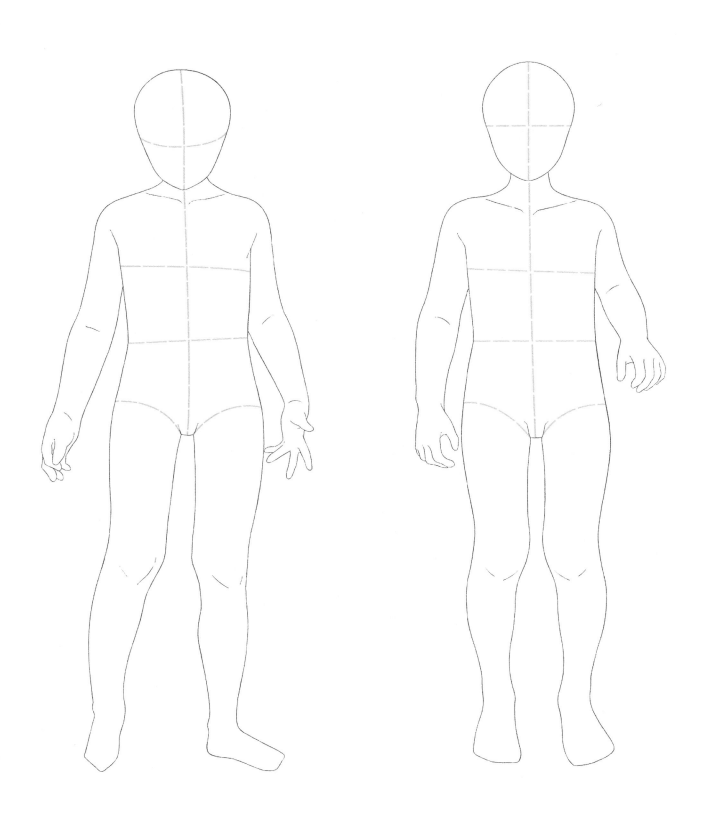

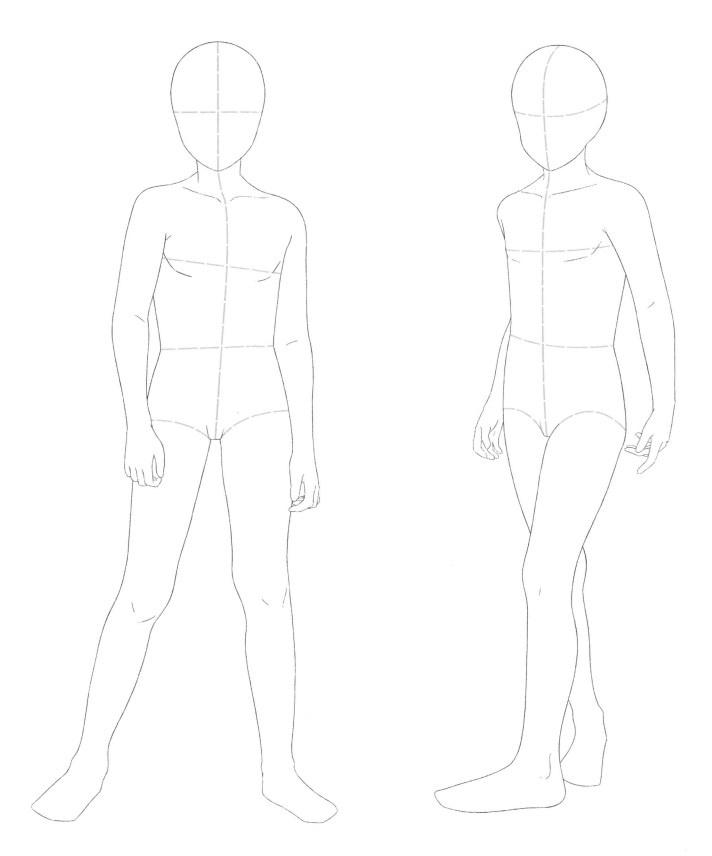

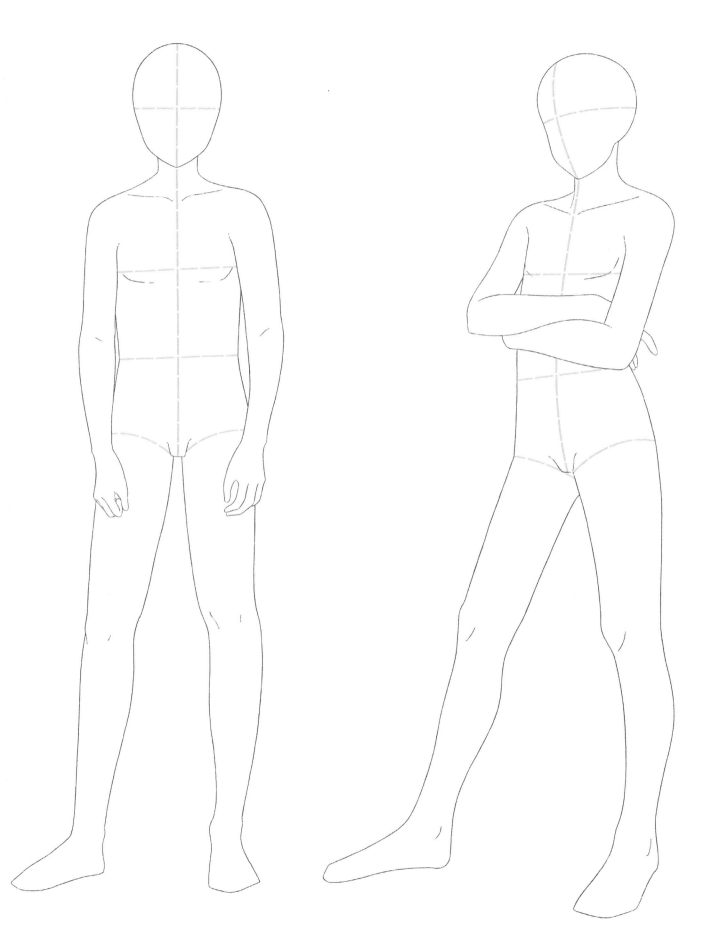

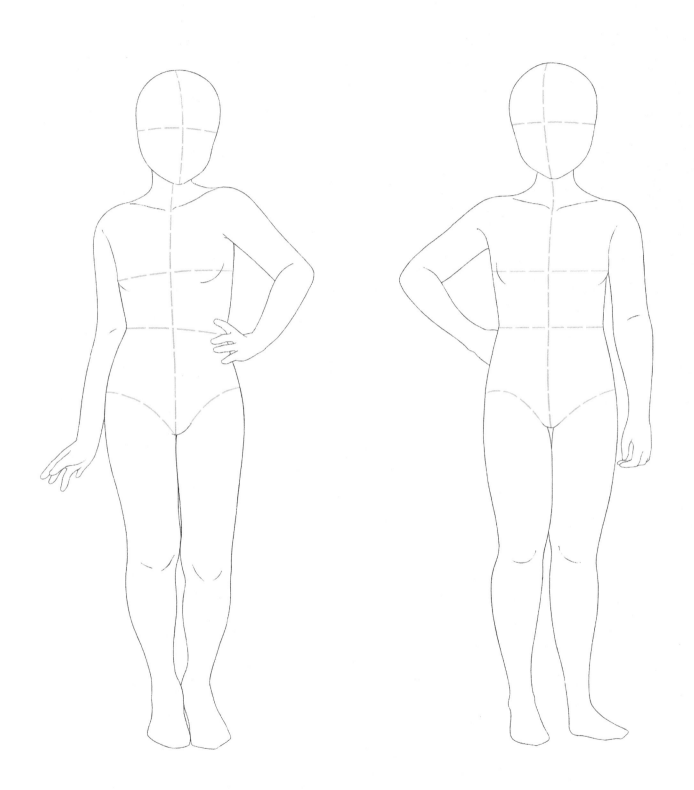

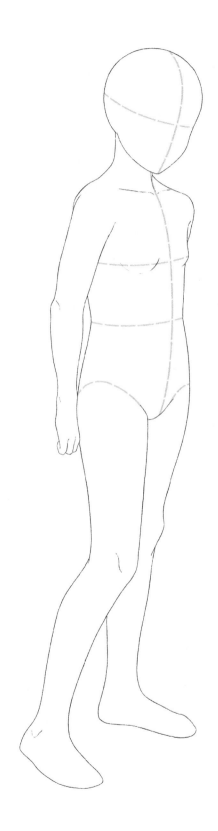
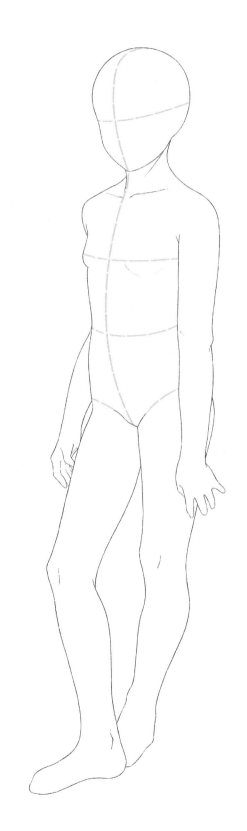

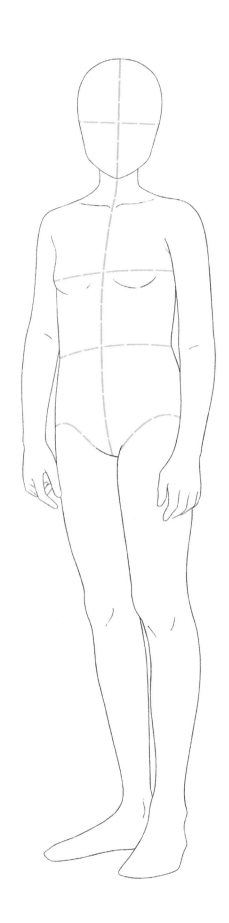
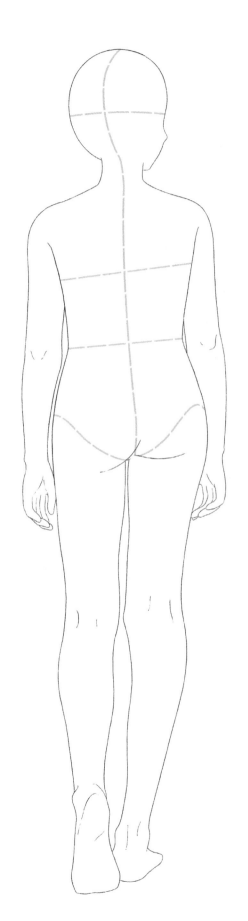

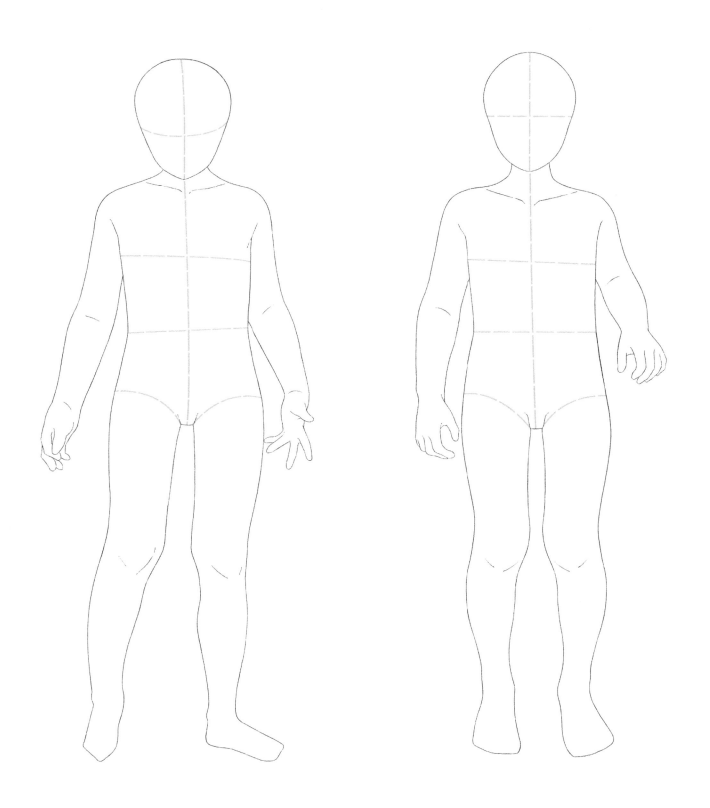

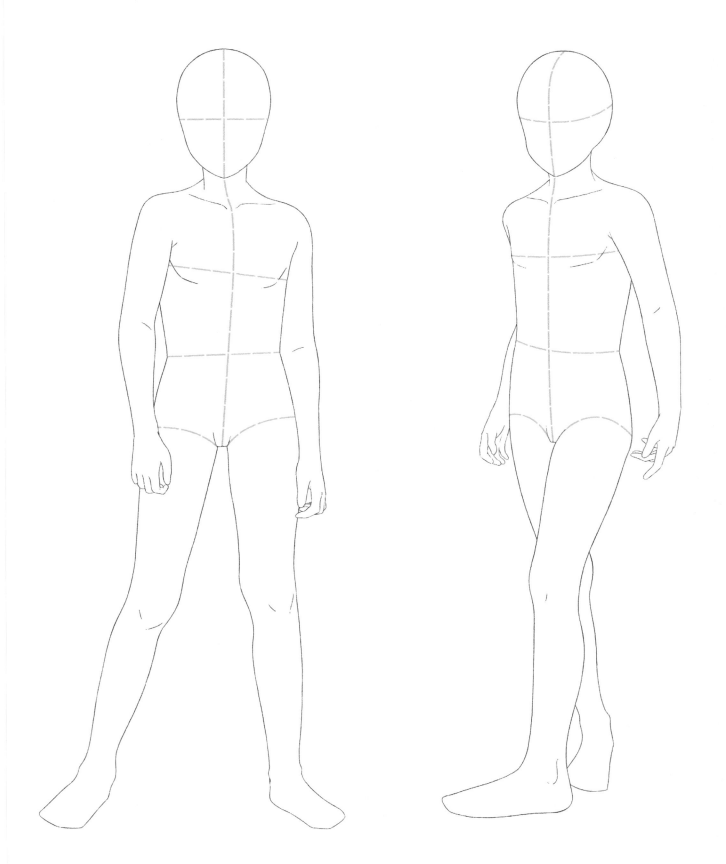

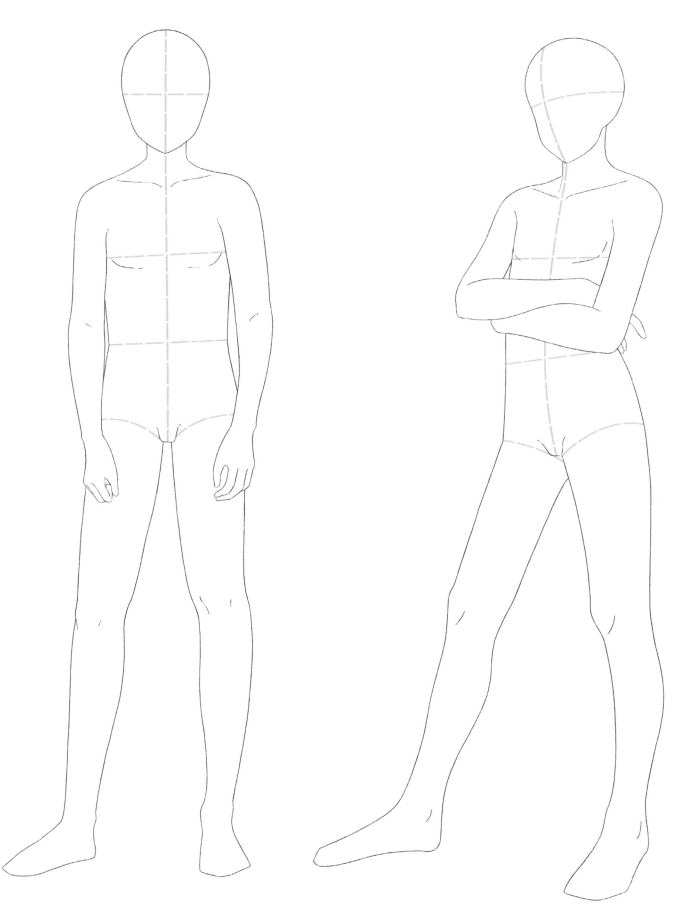

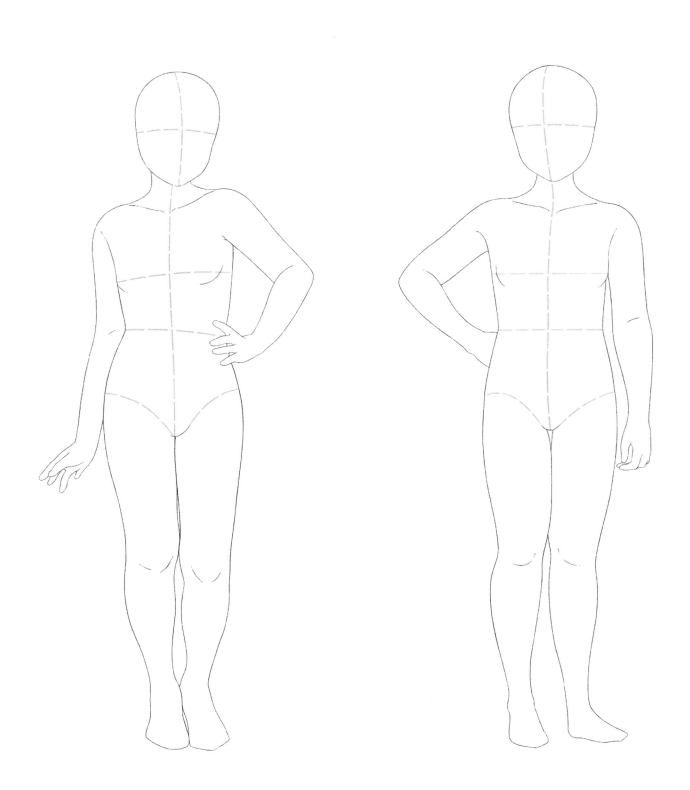

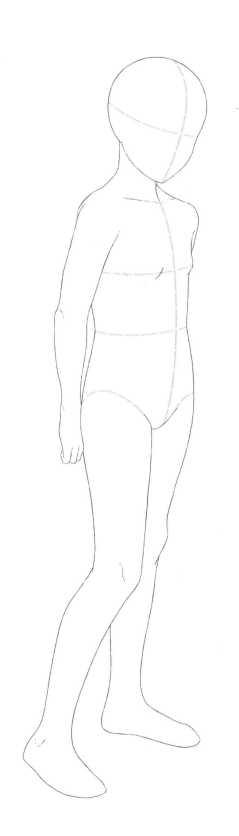
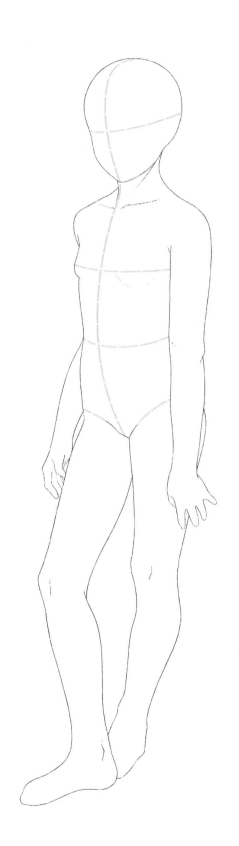

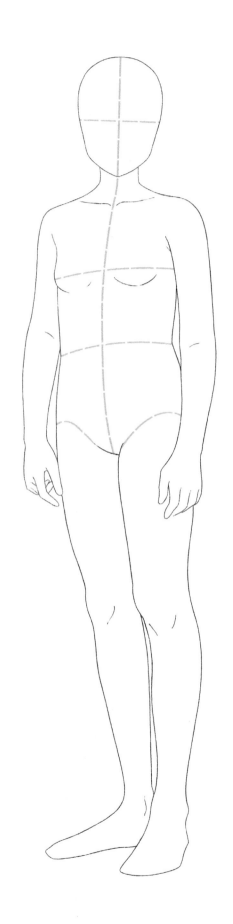
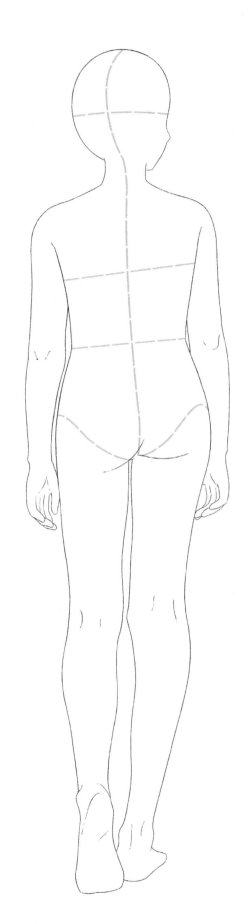

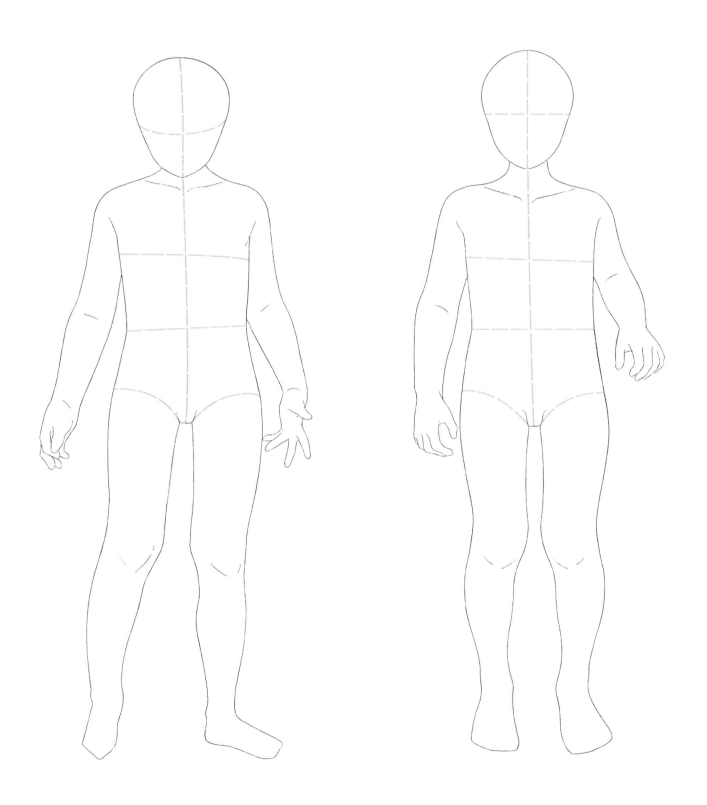

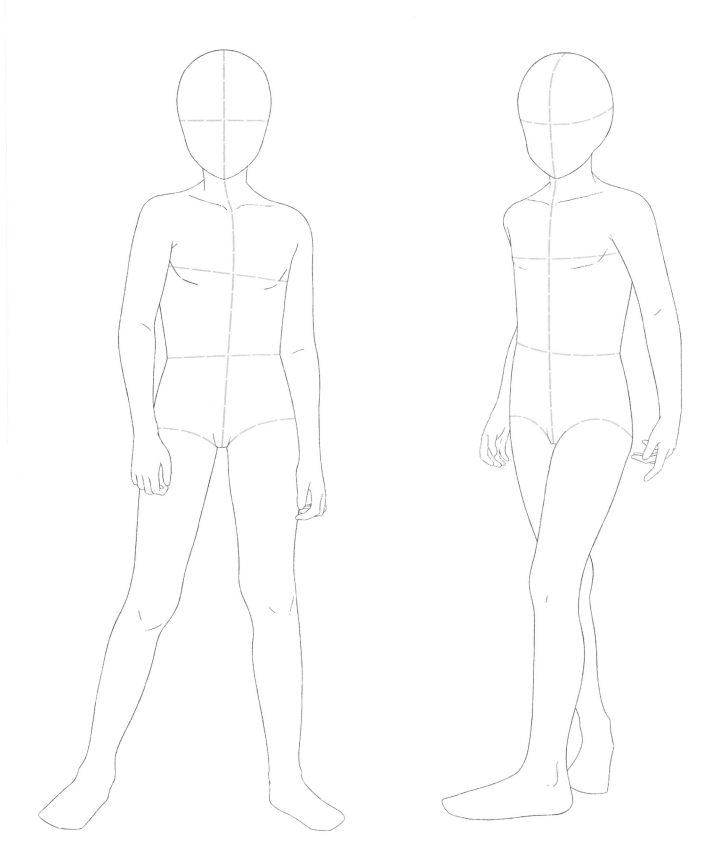

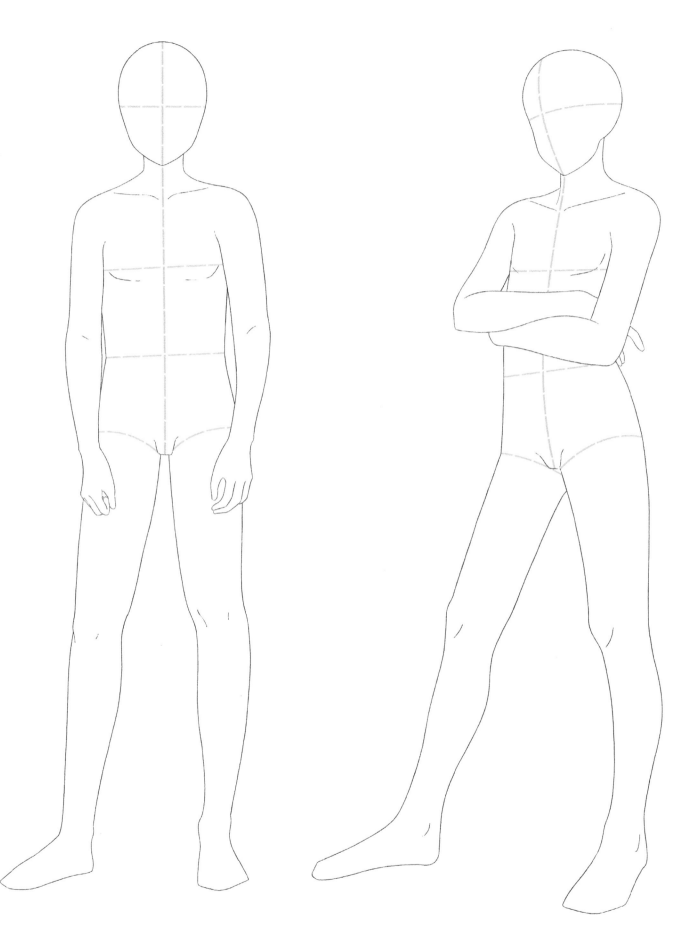

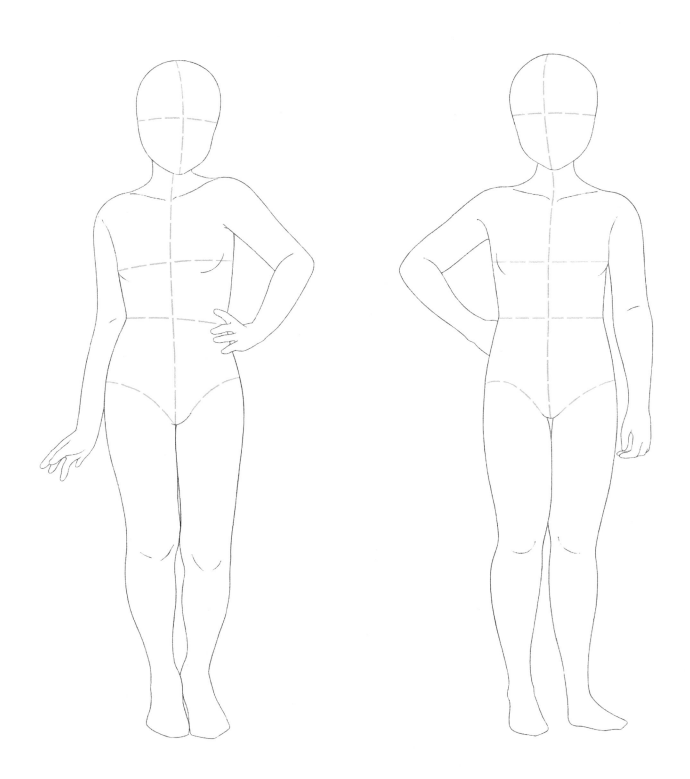

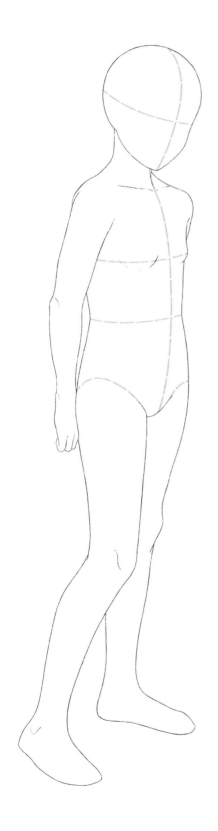
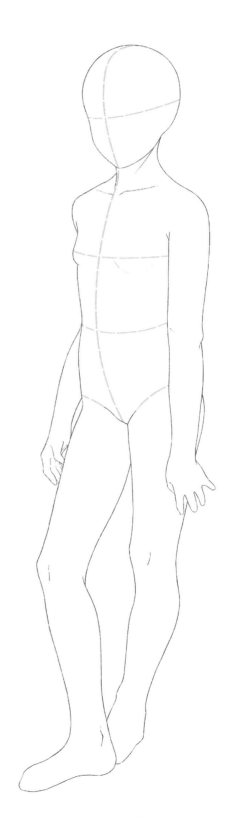

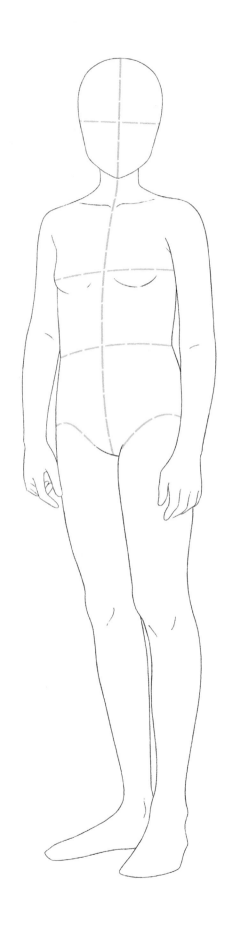
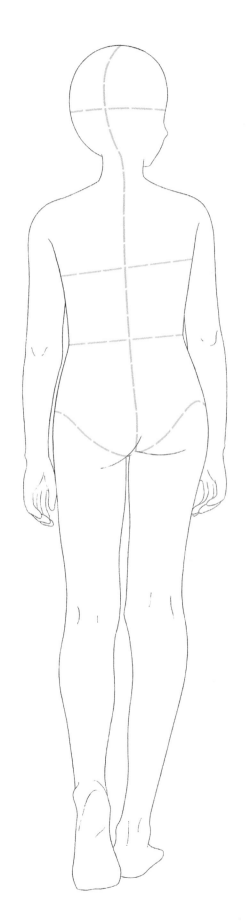

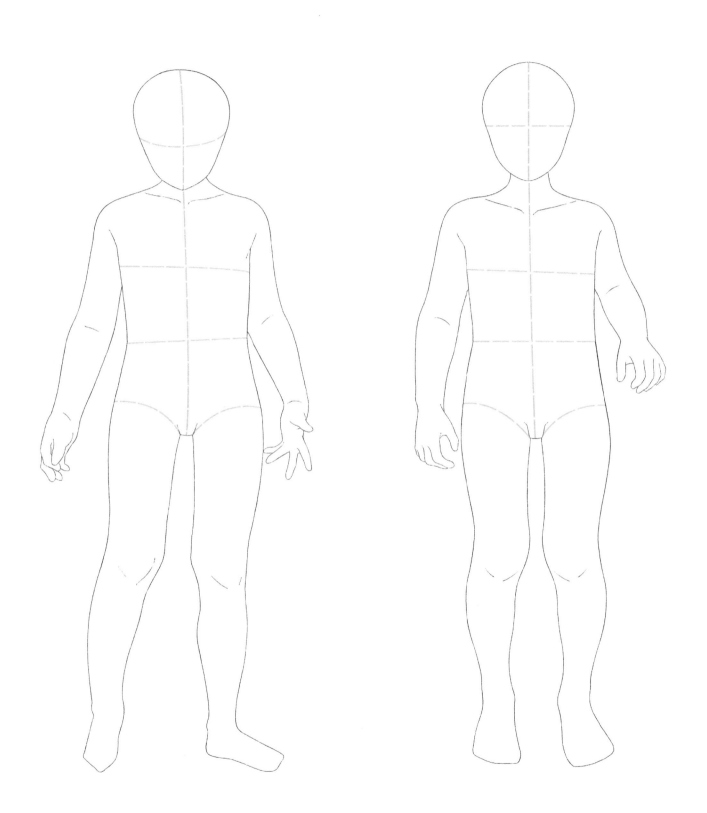

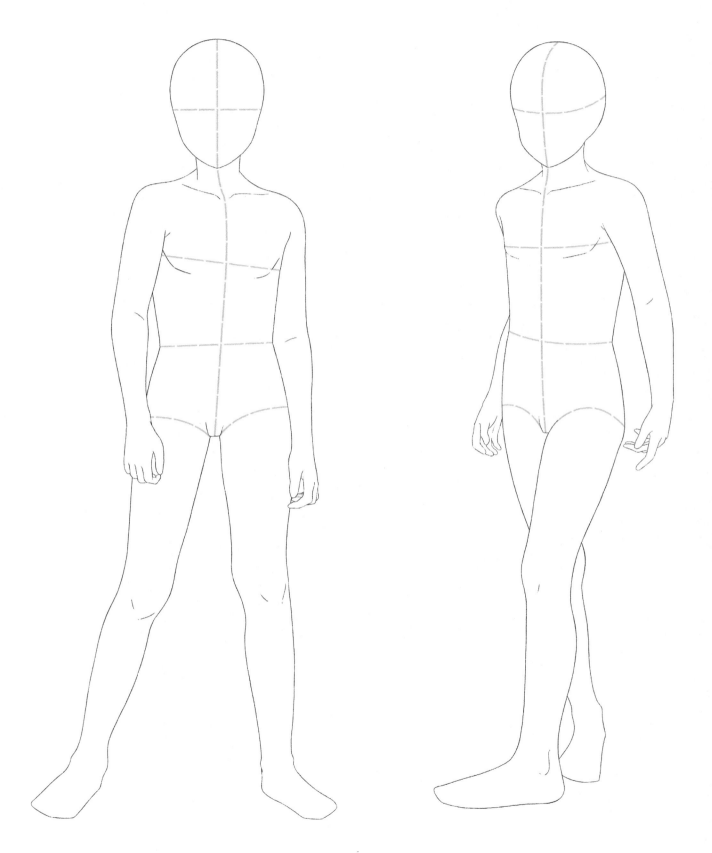

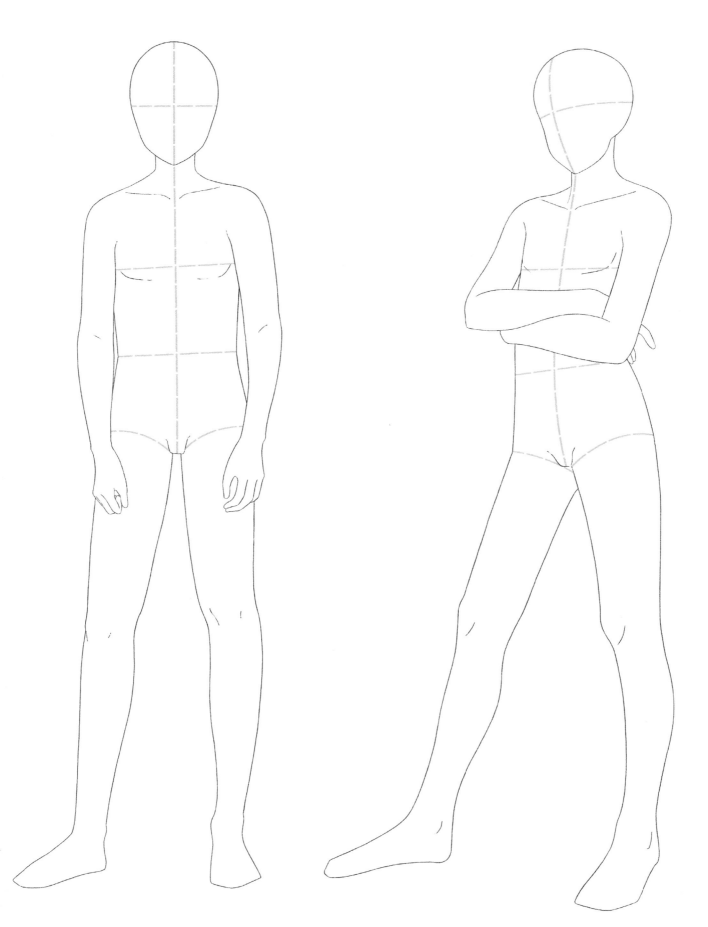

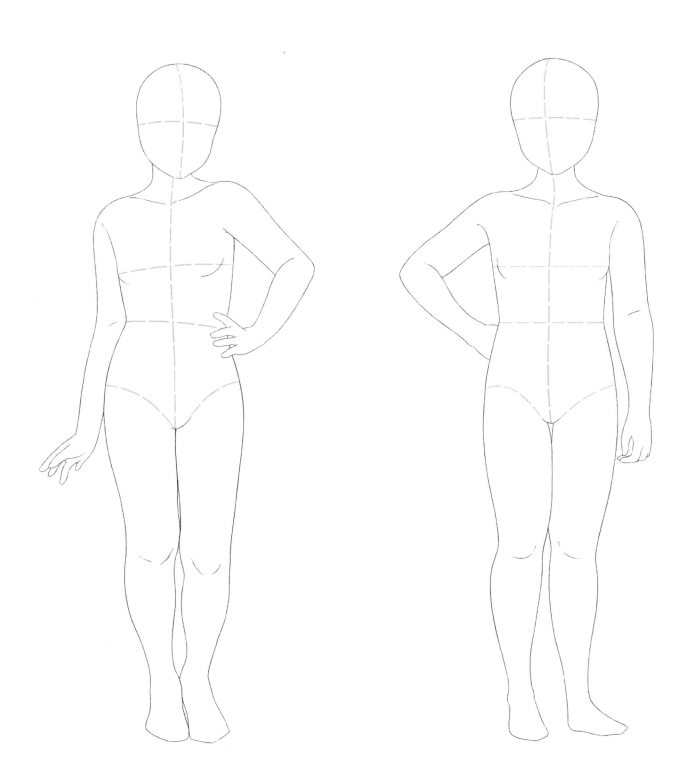

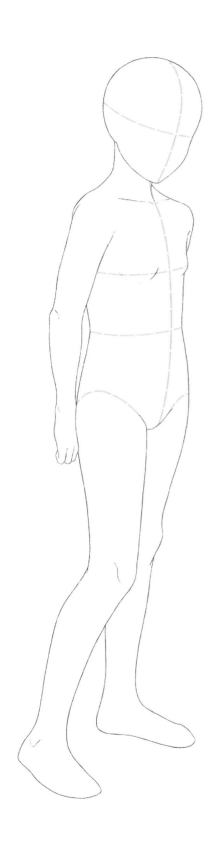
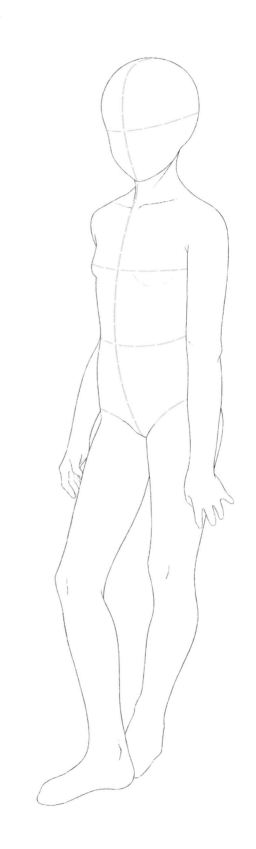

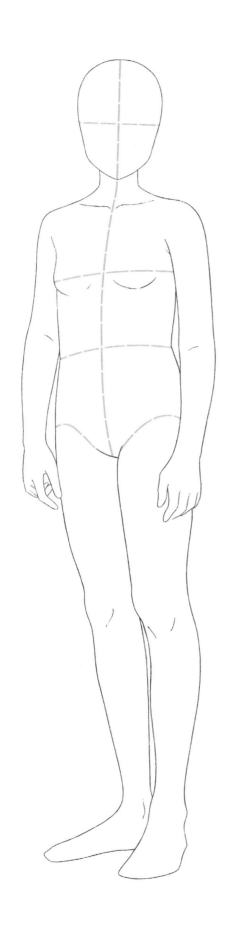
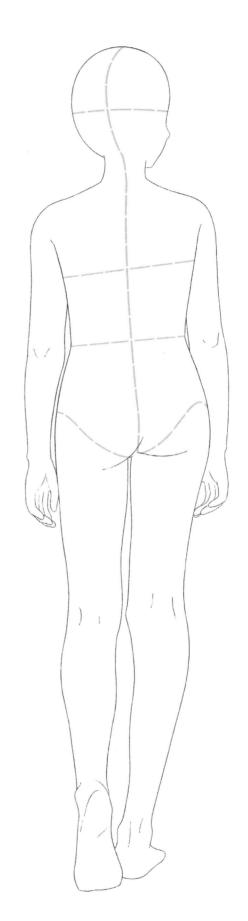

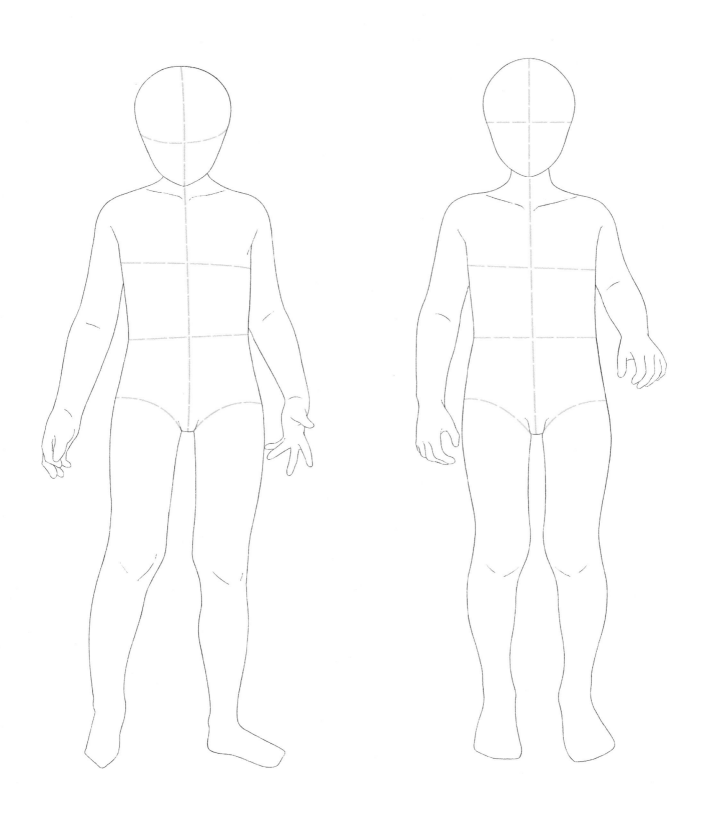

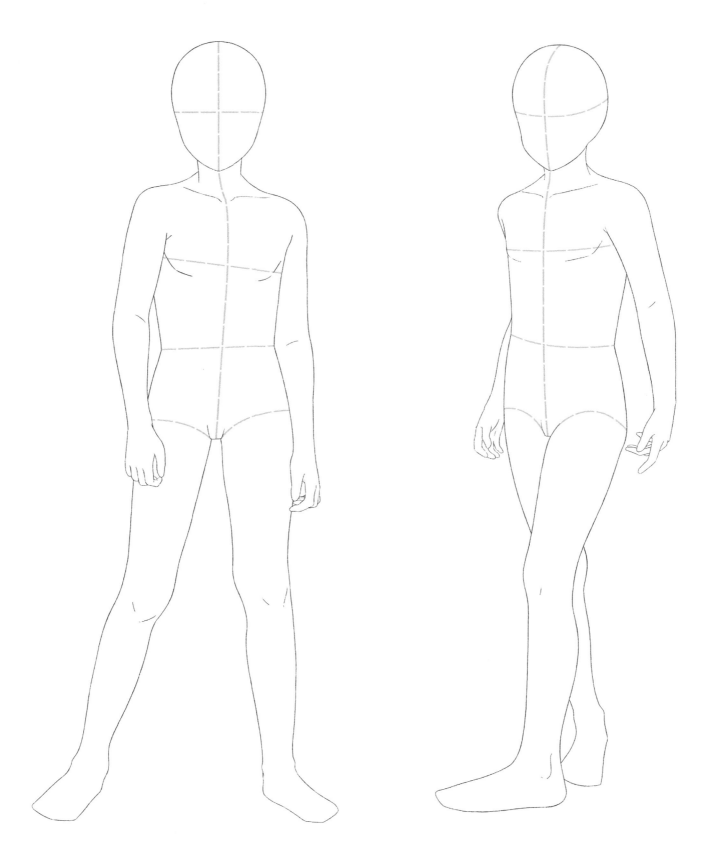

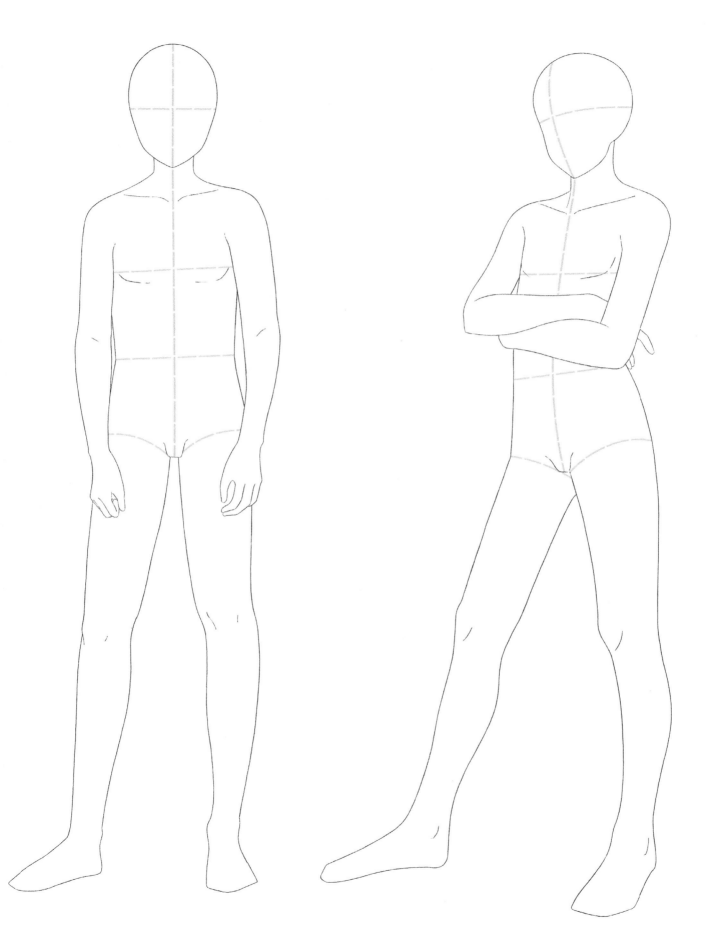

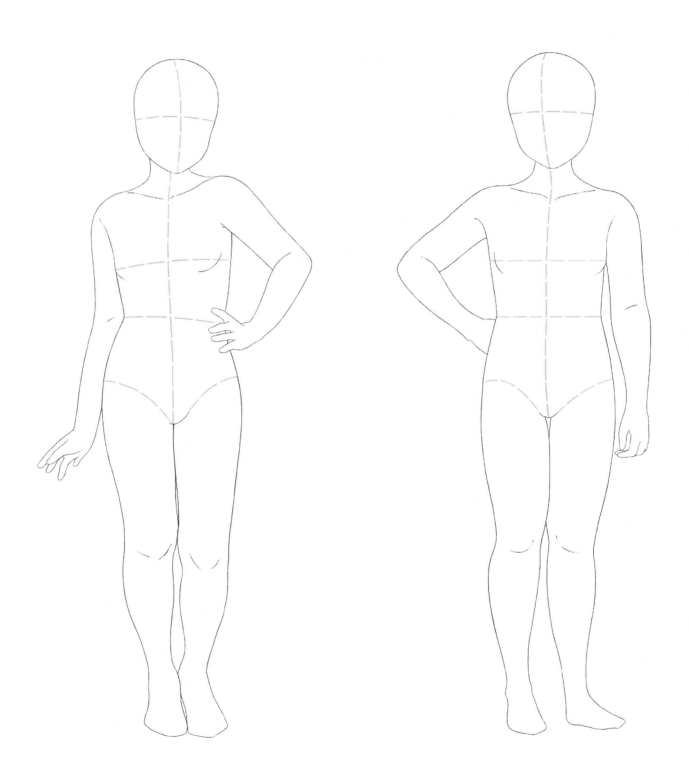

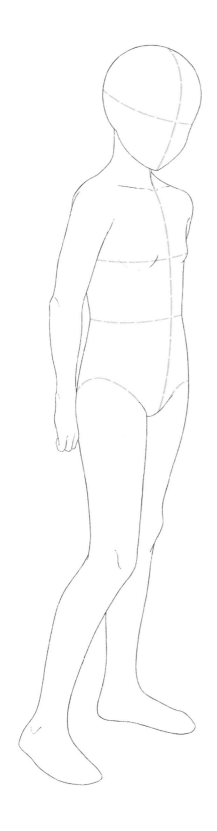
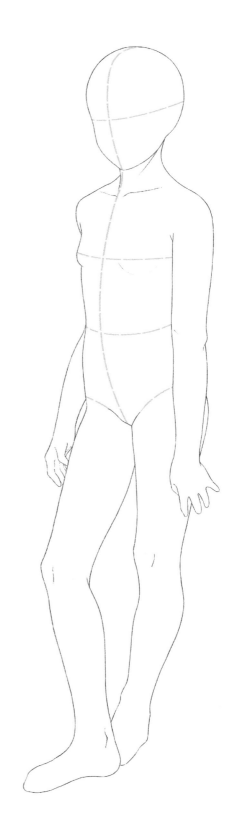

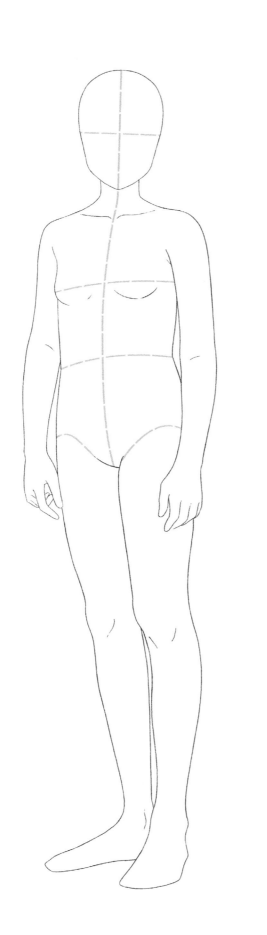
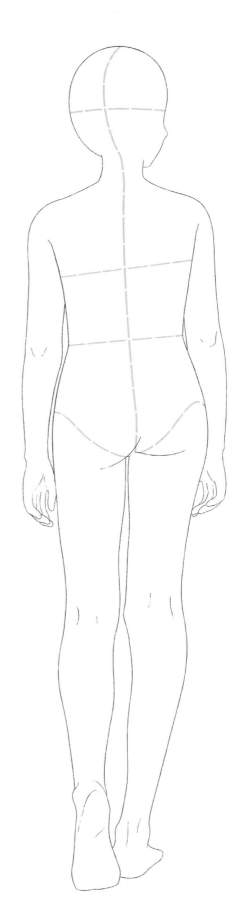

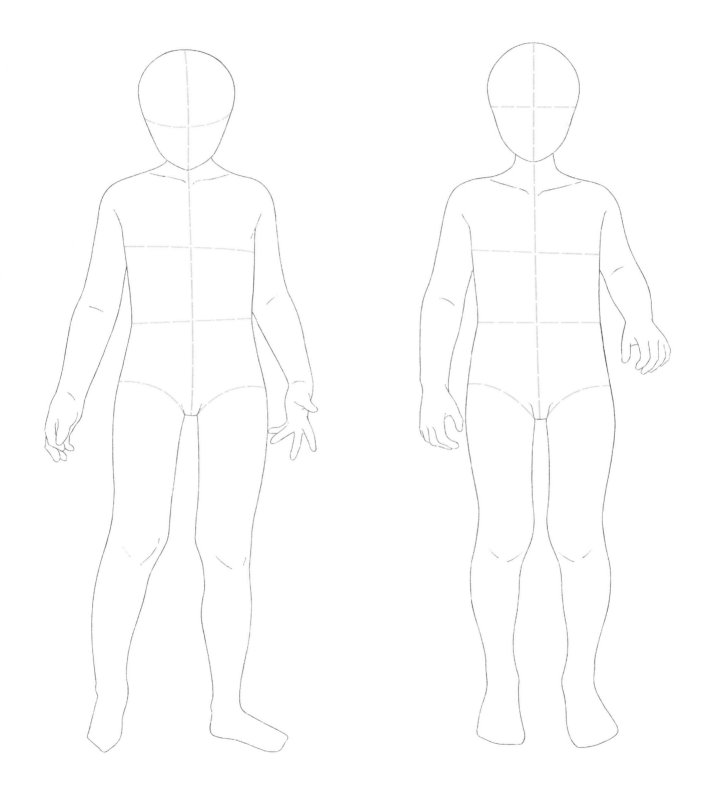

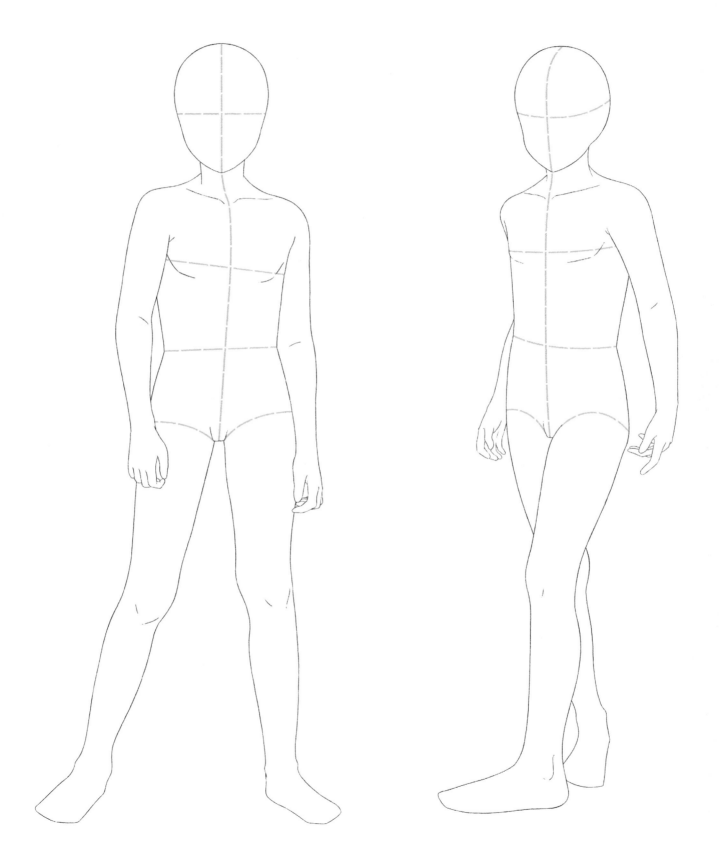

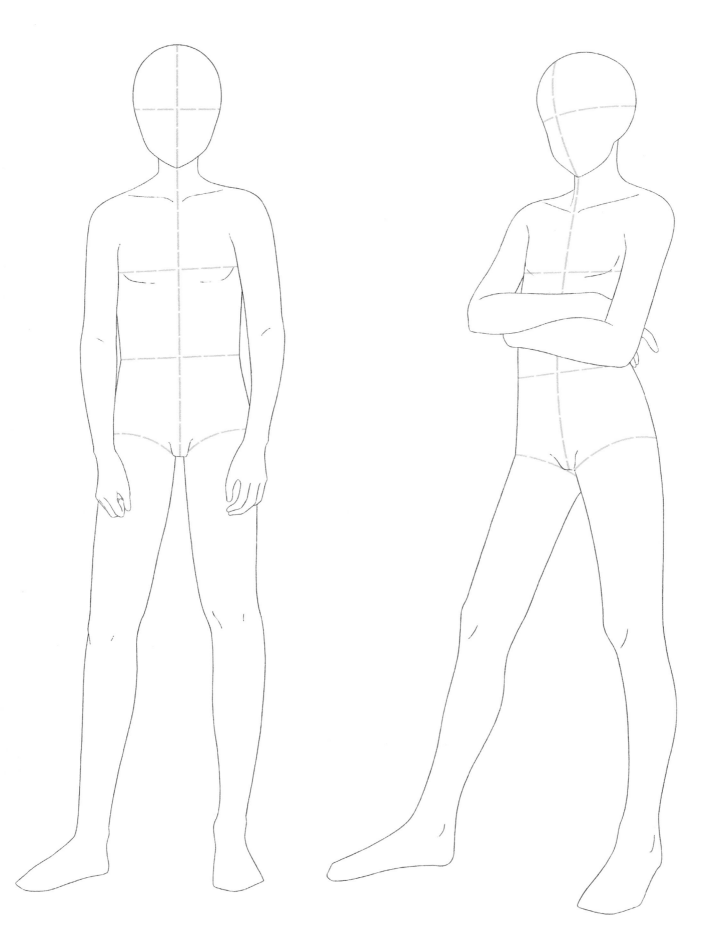

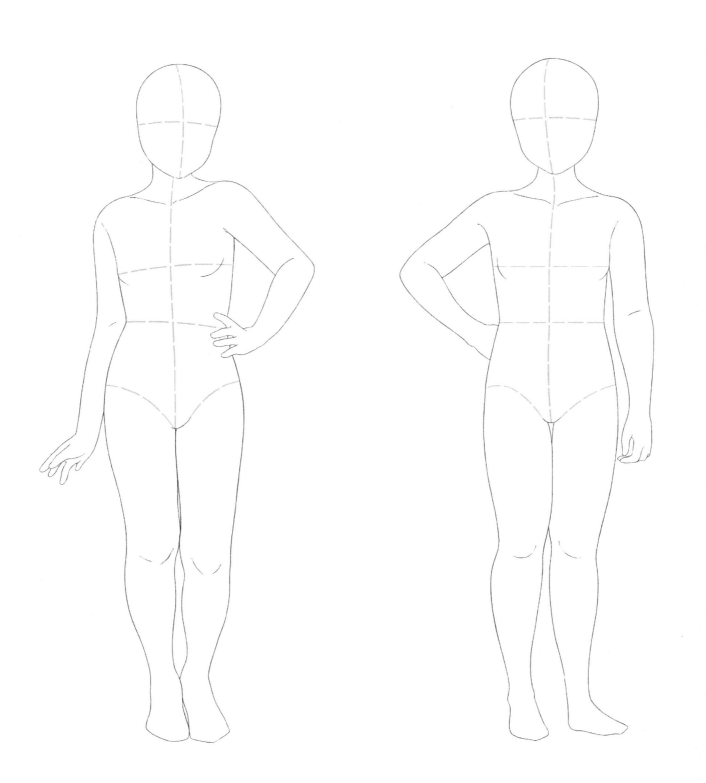

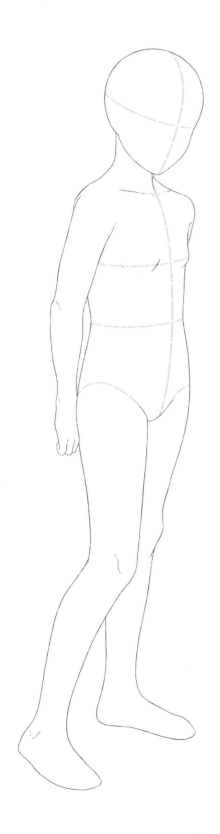
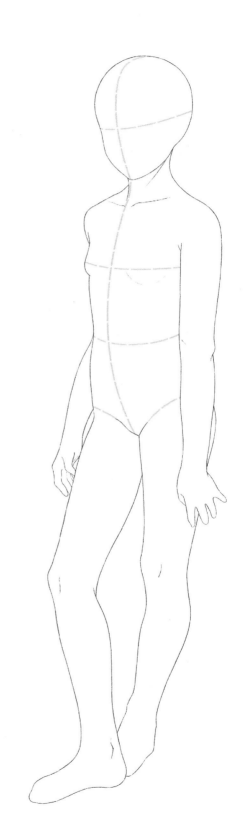

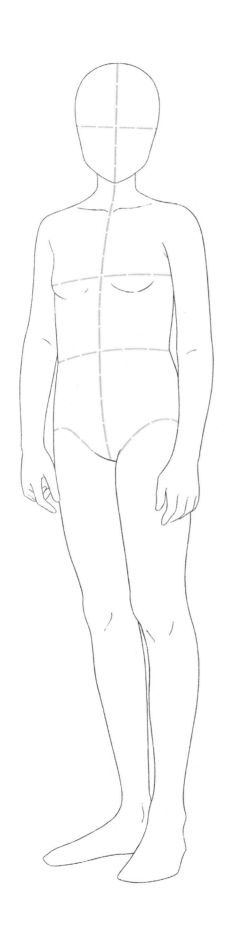
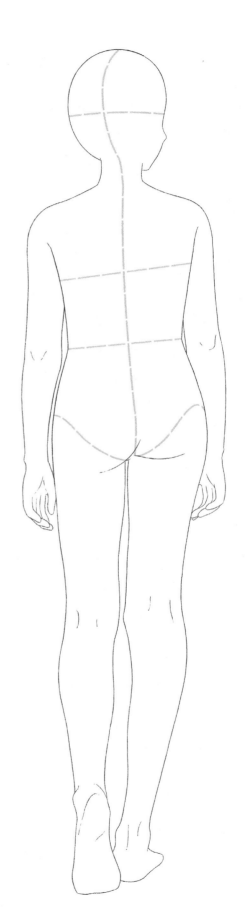

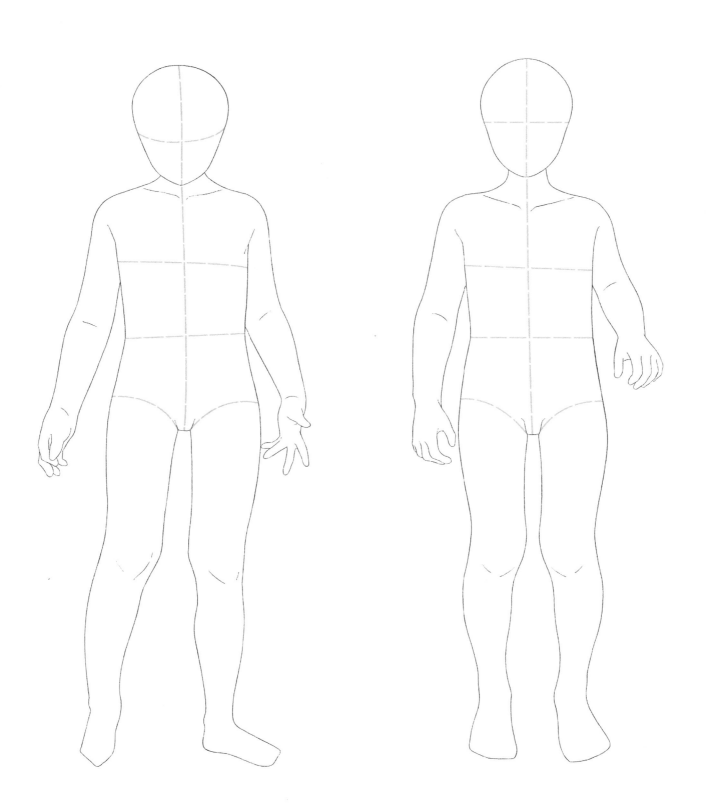

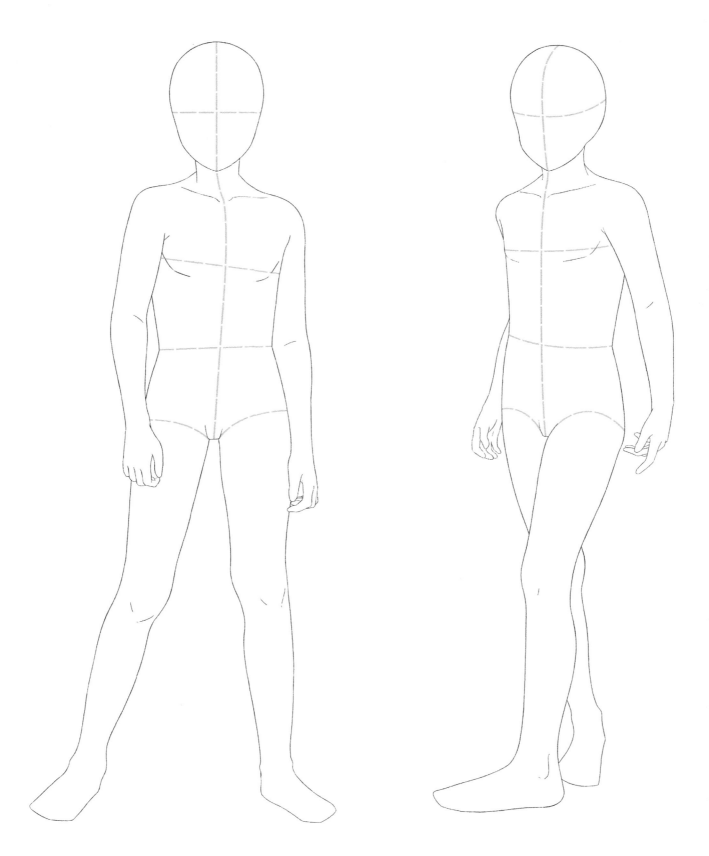

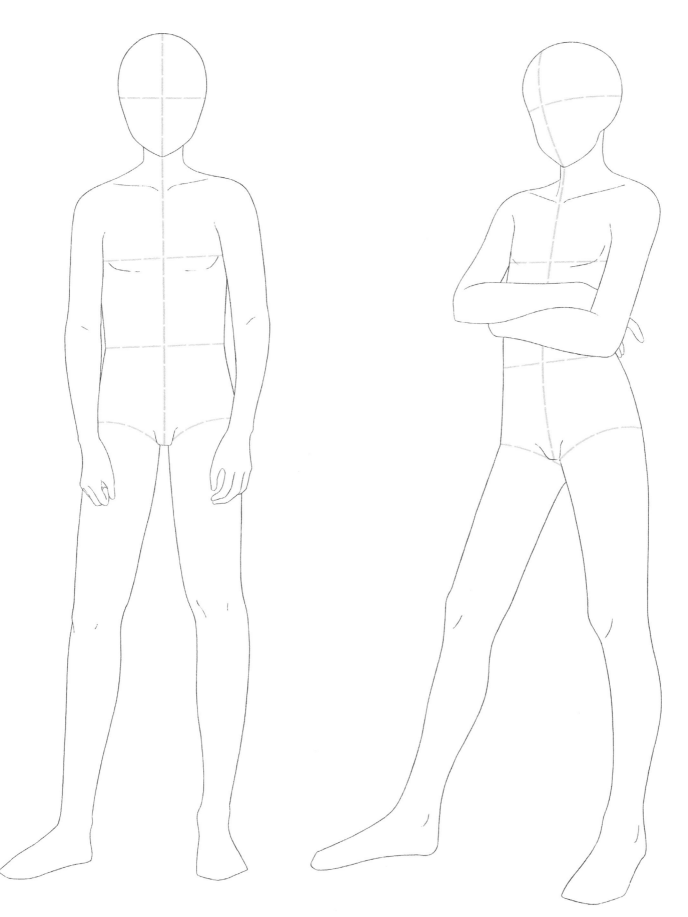

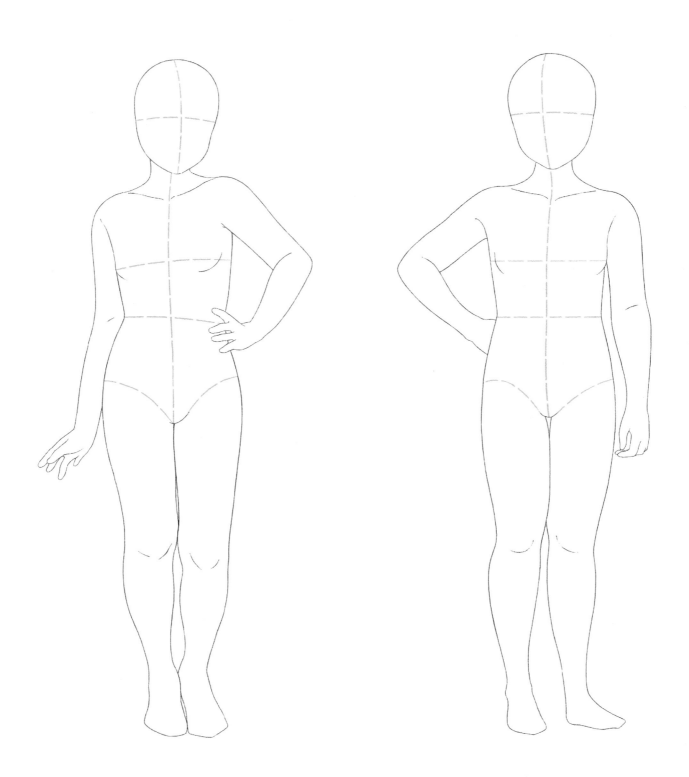

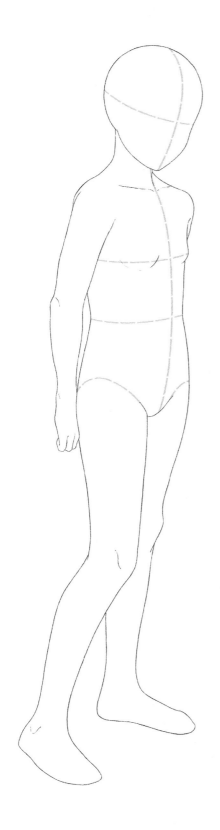
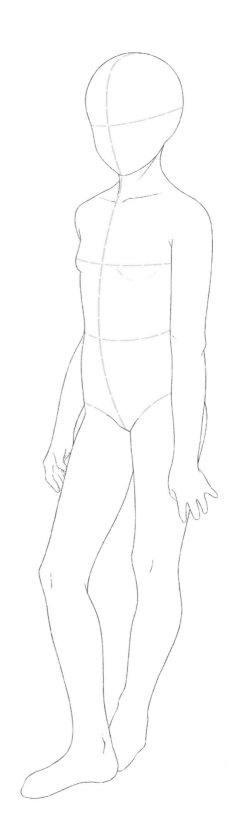

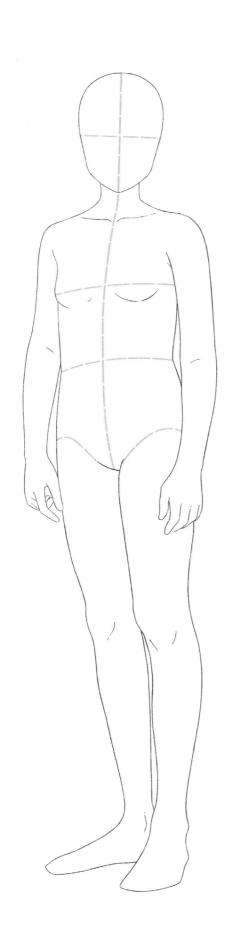
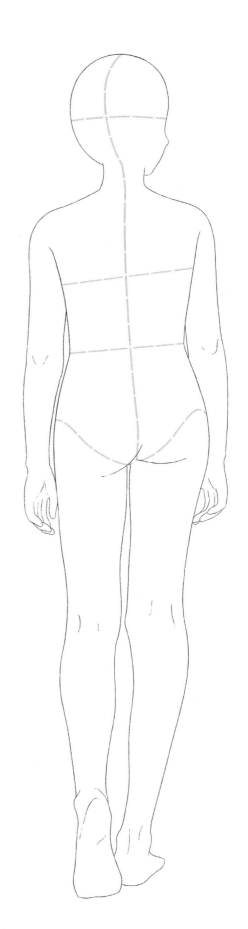

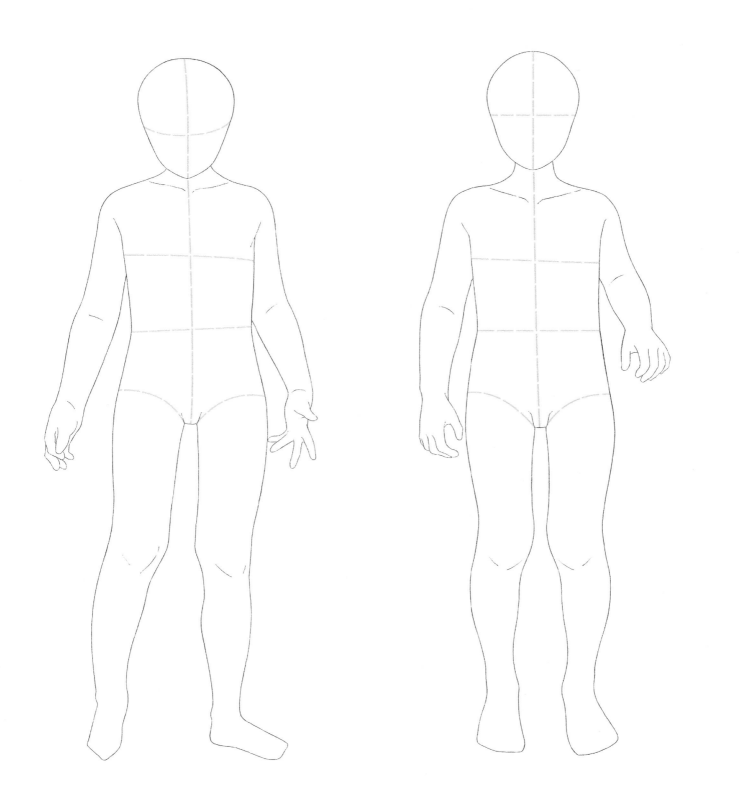

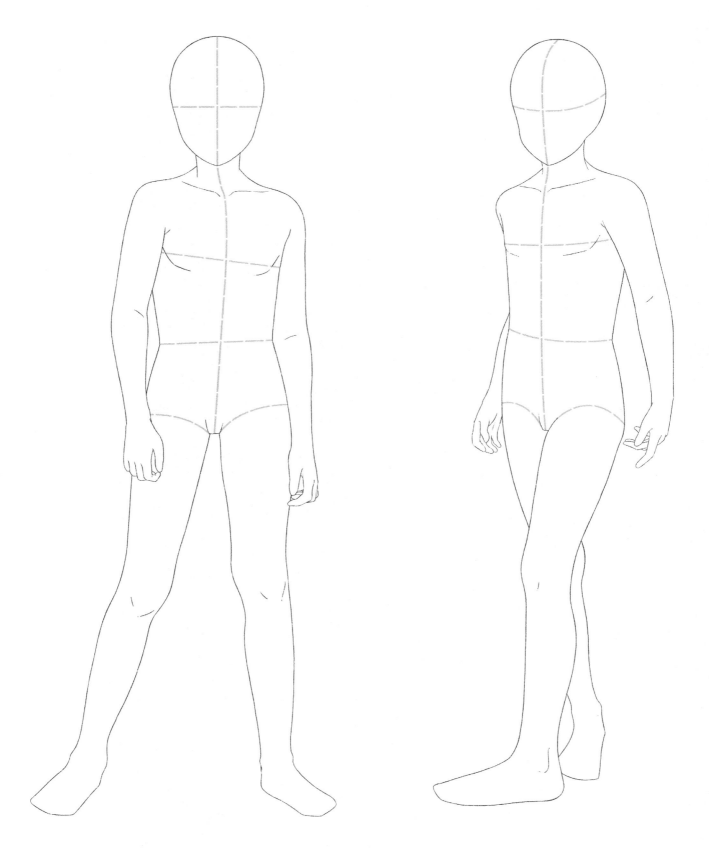

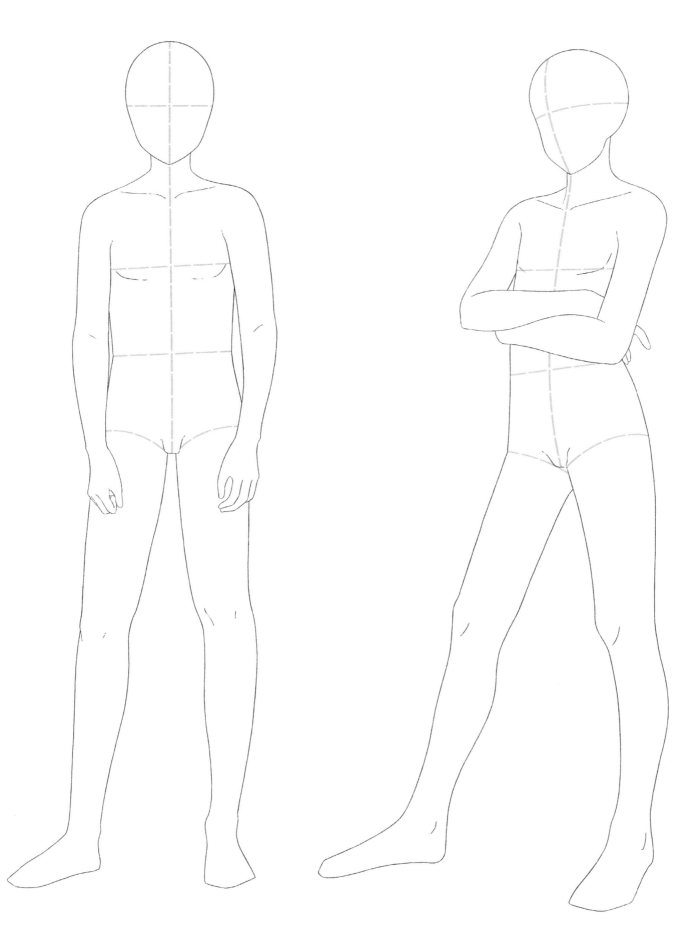

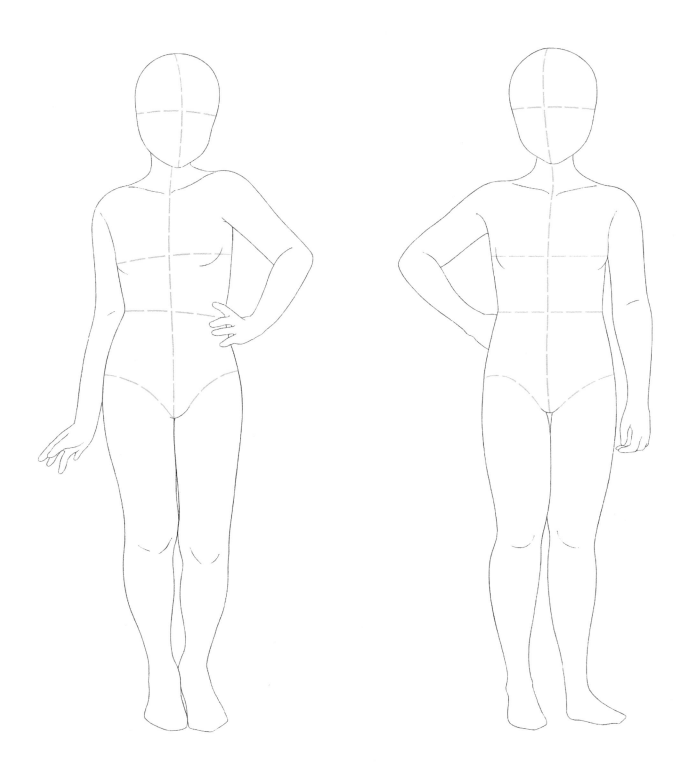

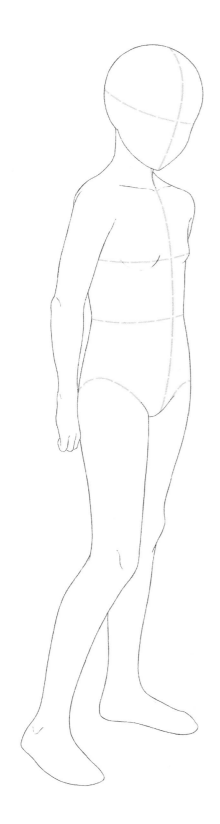
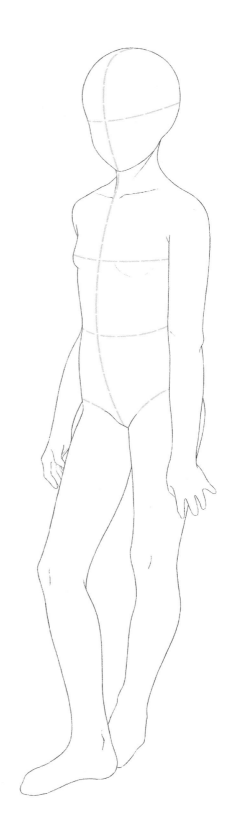

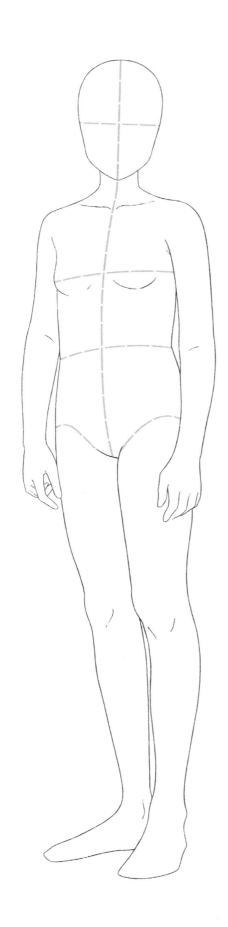
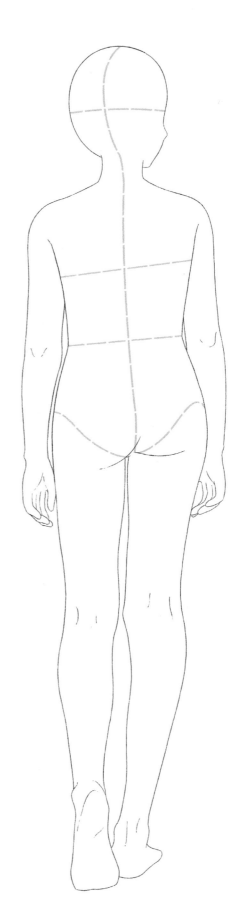

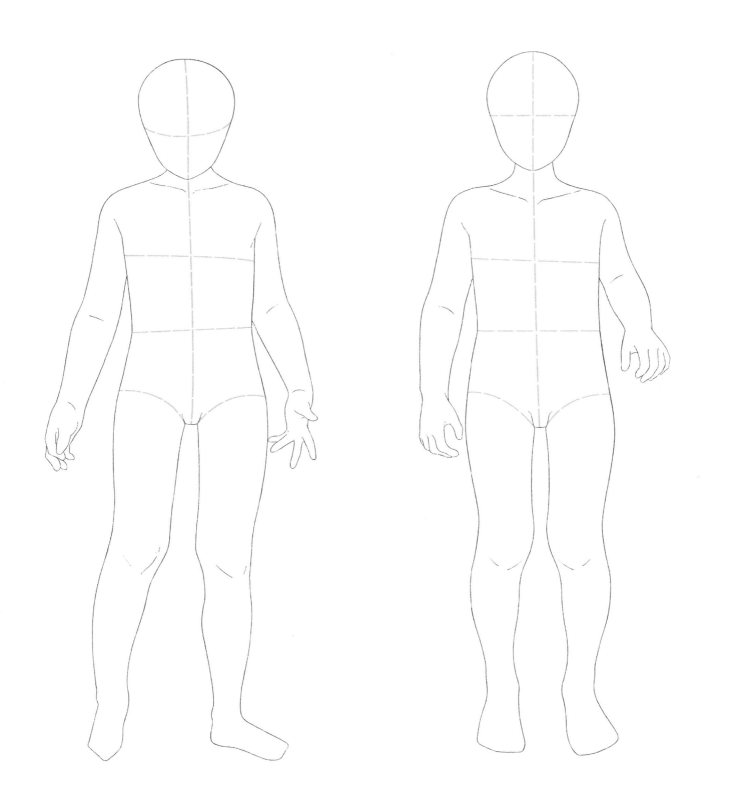

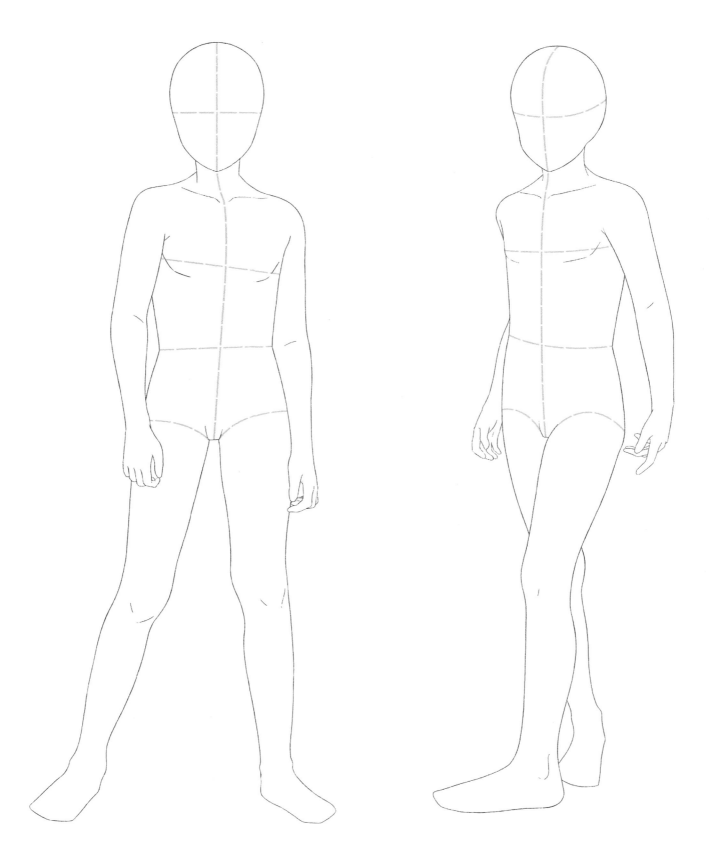

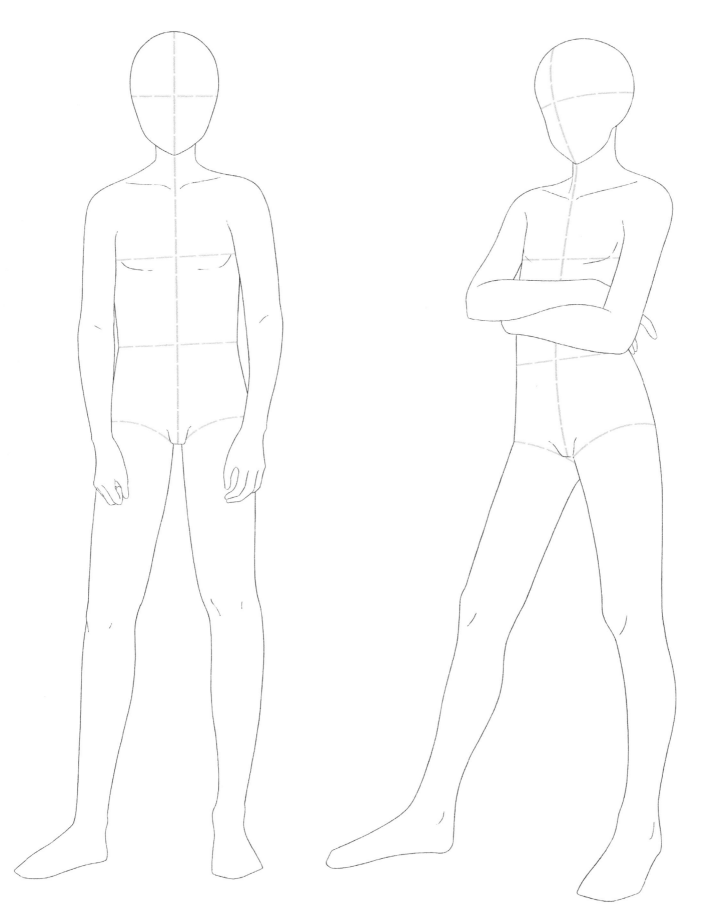

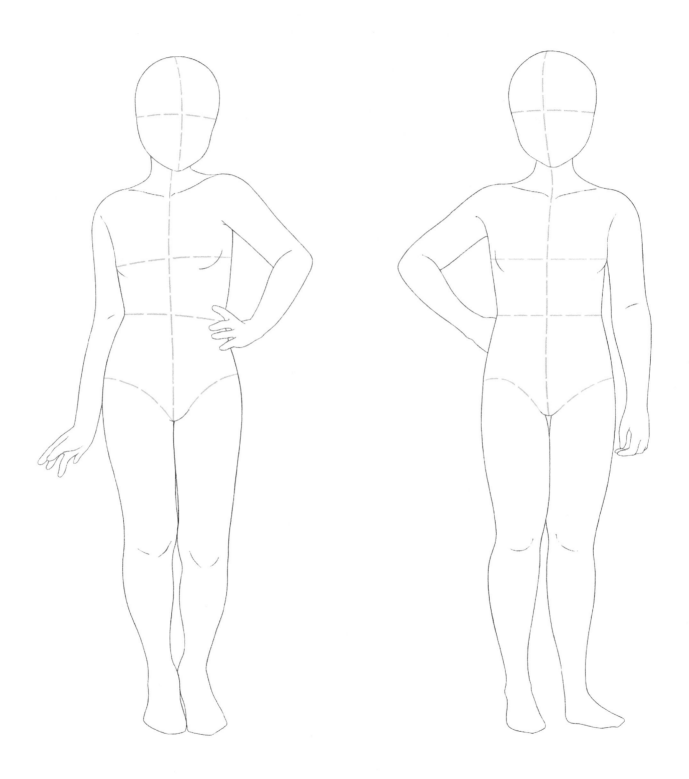

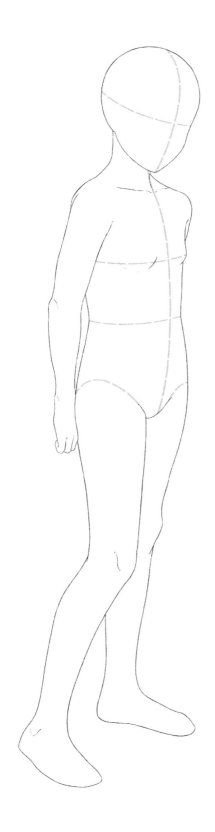
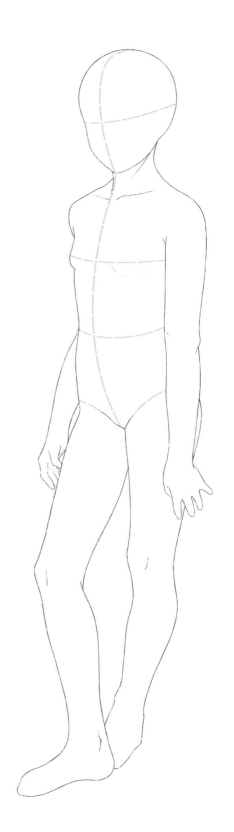

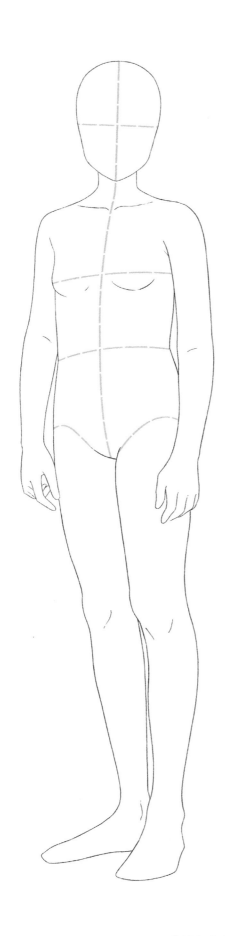
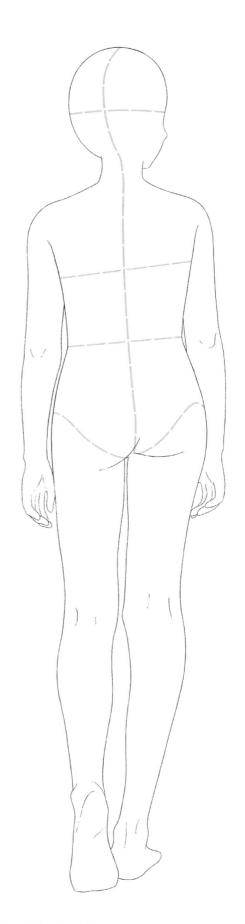

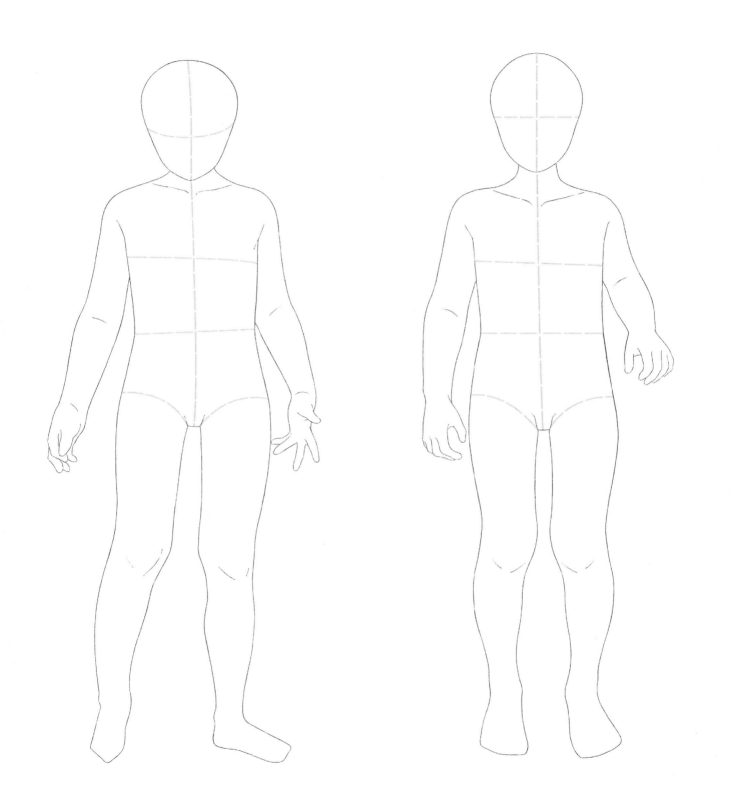

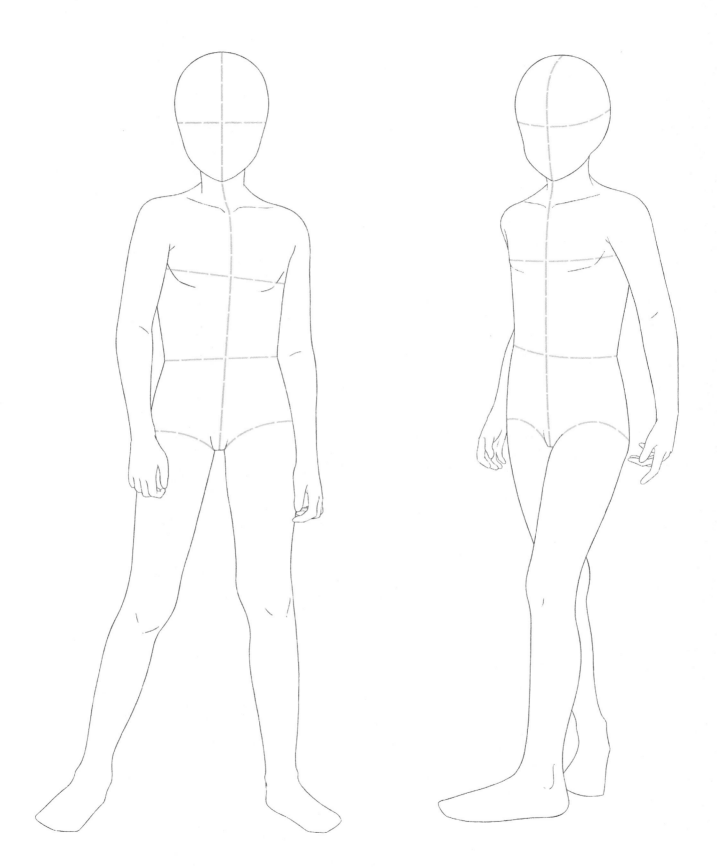

BOY'S FASHION FIGURINE | 6-8 YEARS

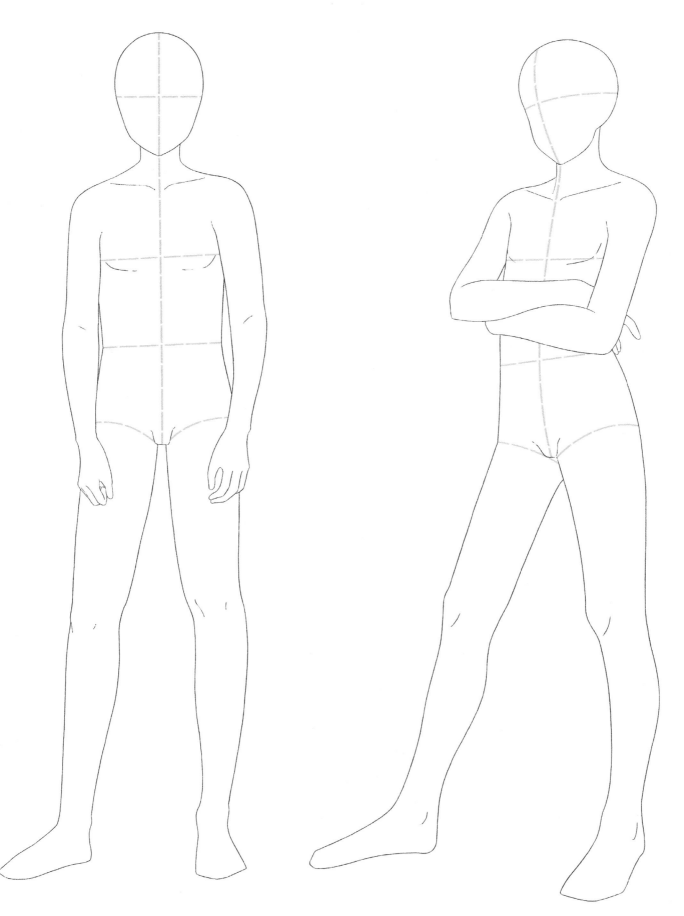

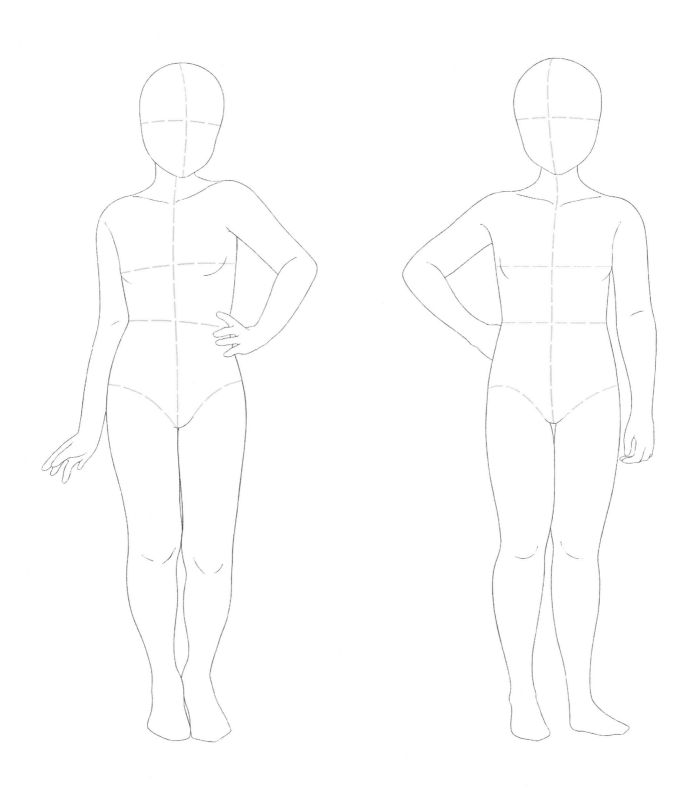

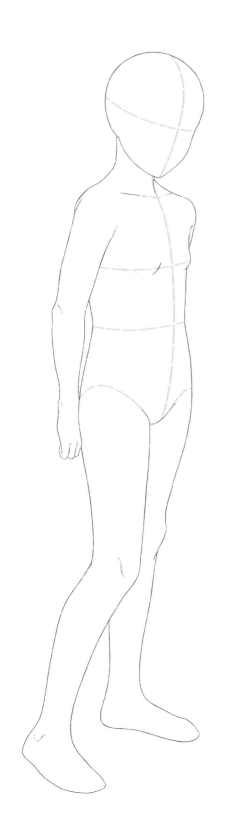
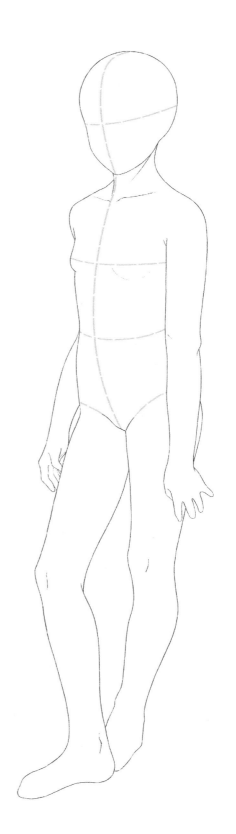

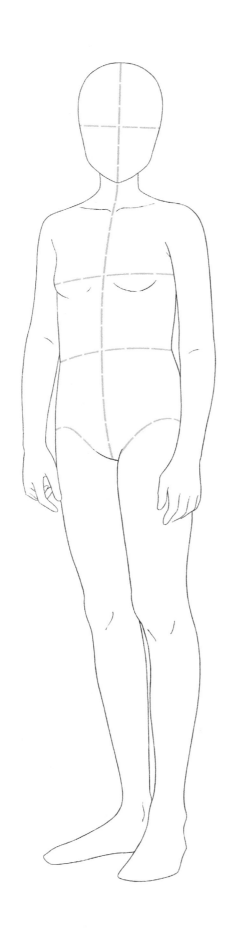
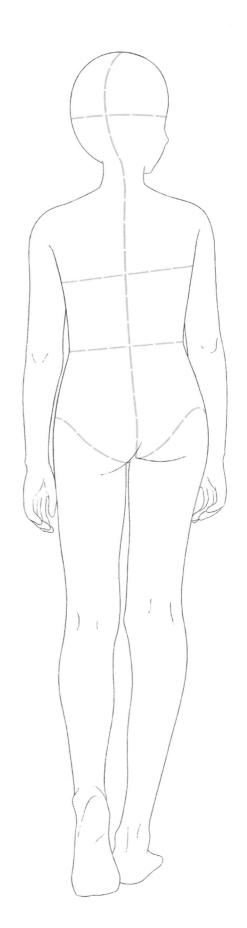

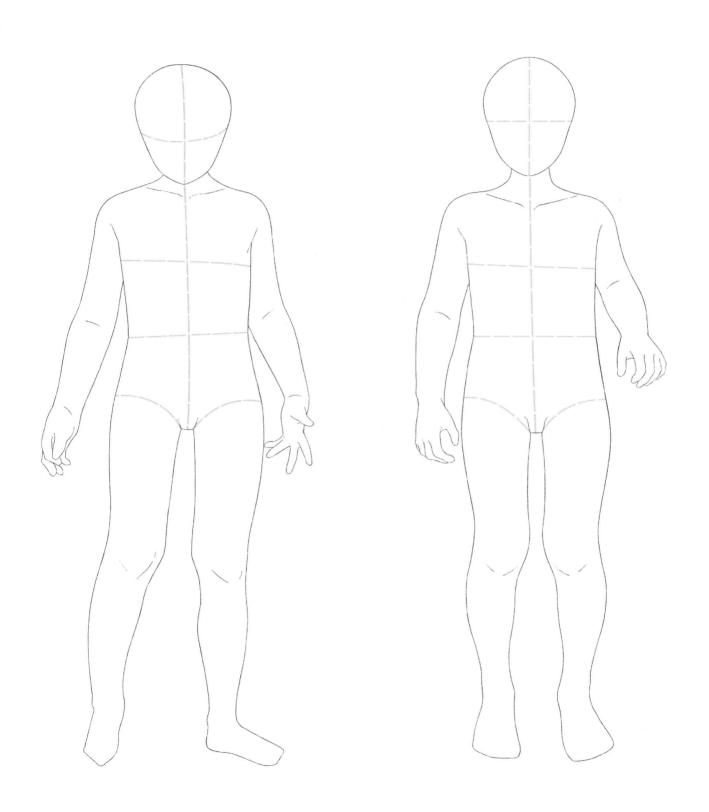

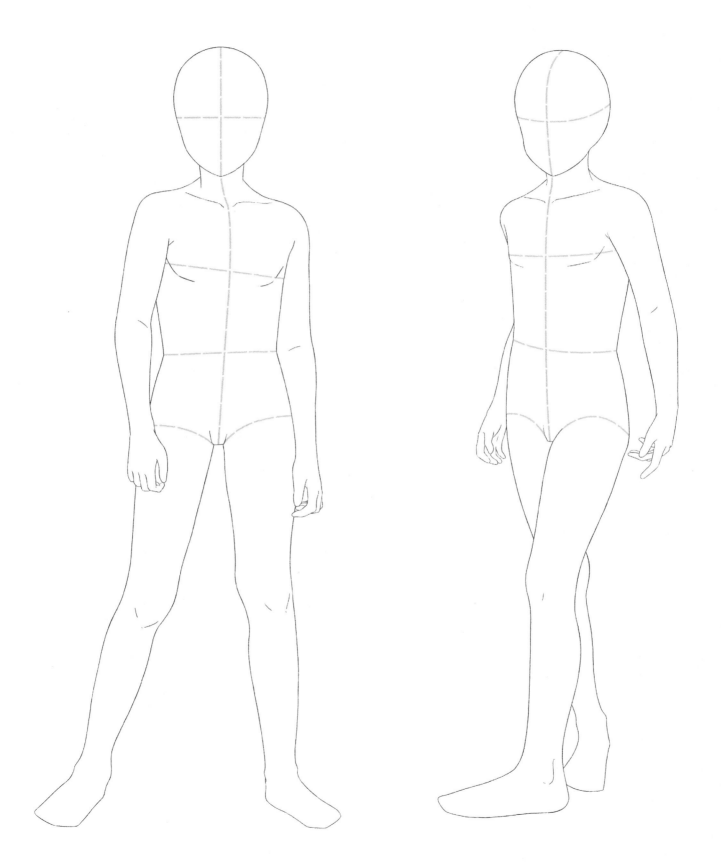

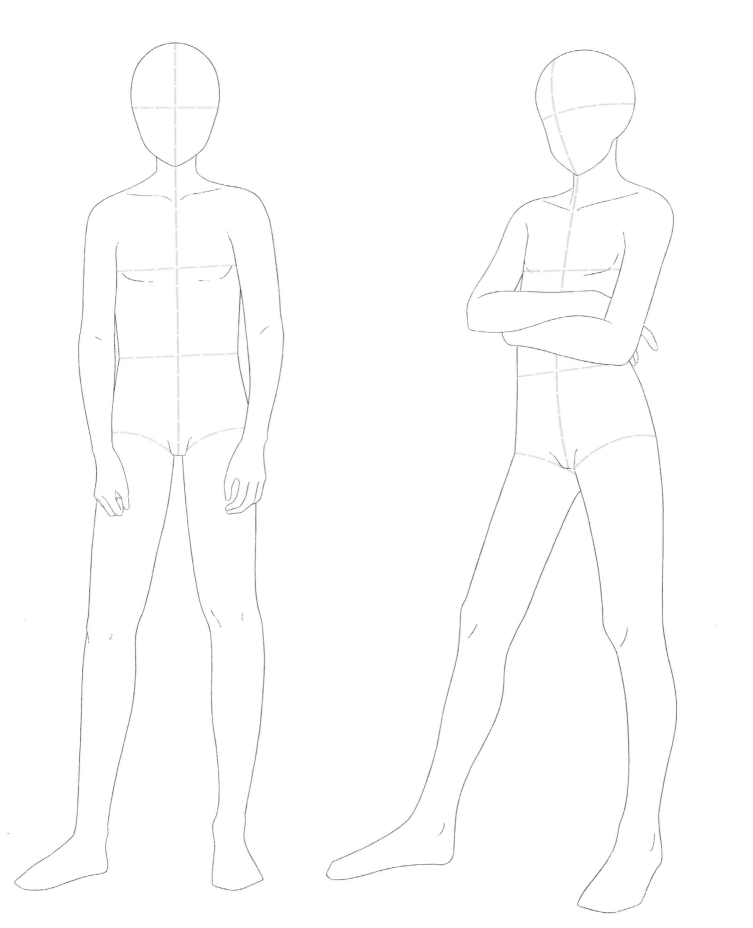

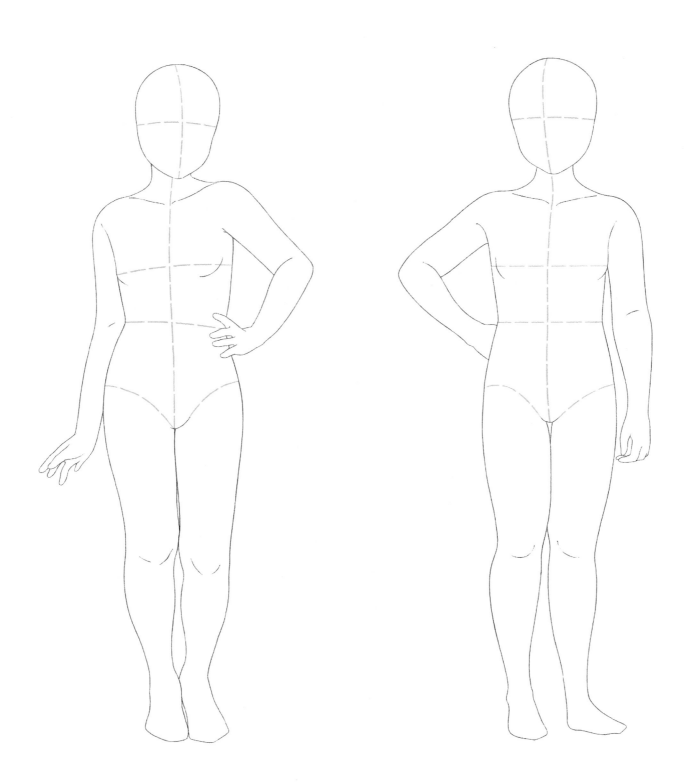

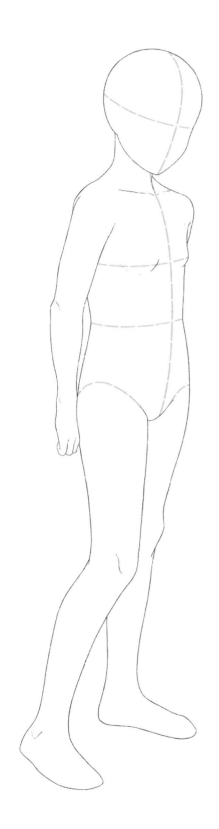
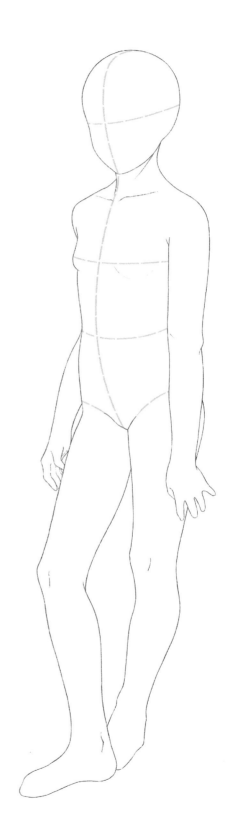

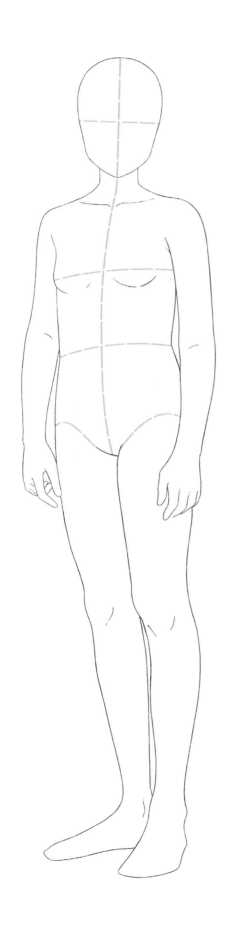
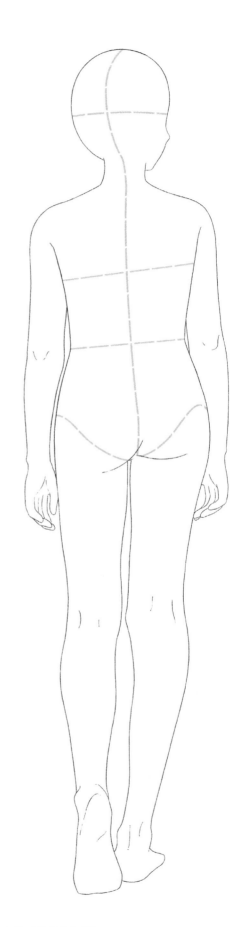

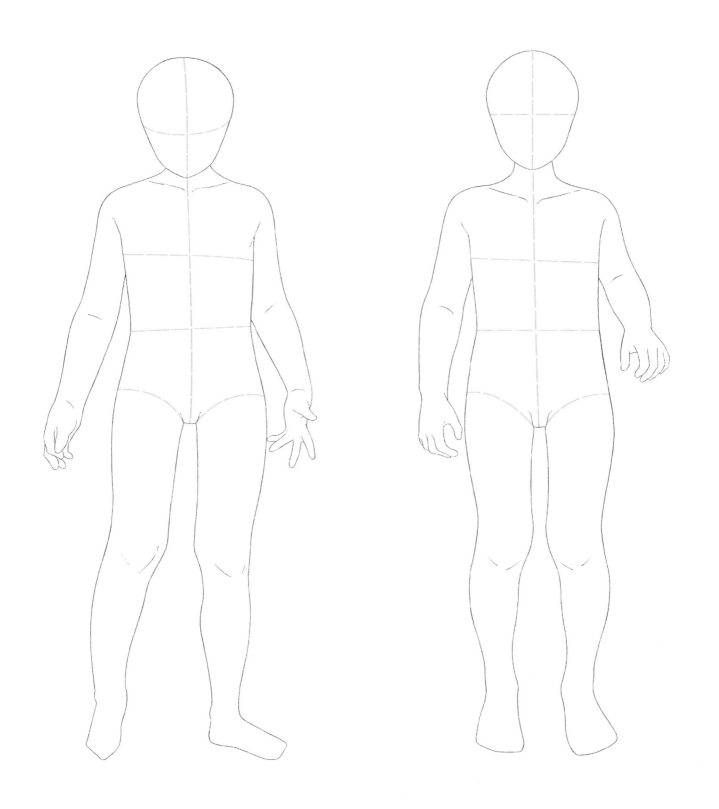

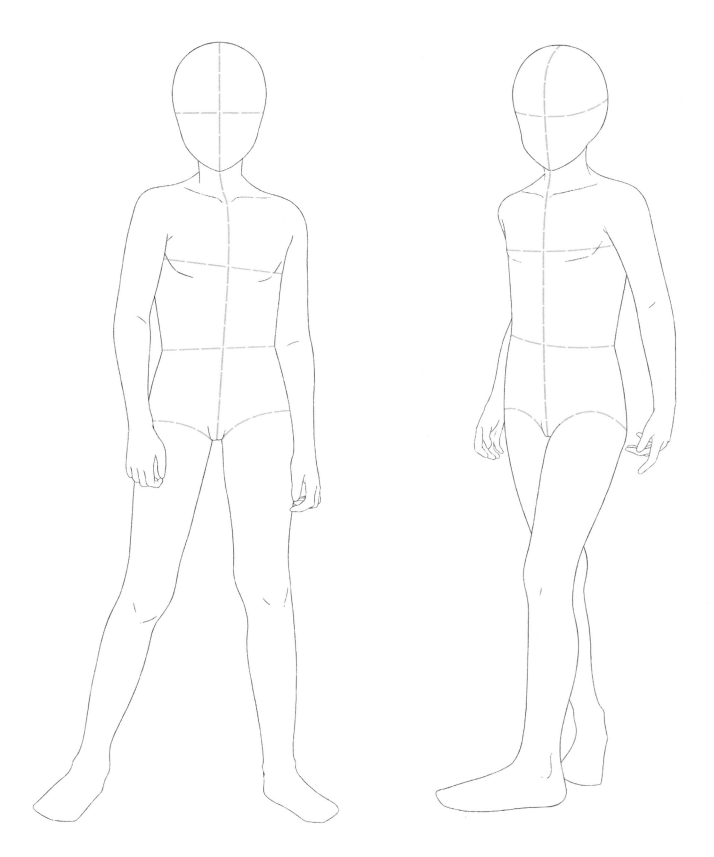

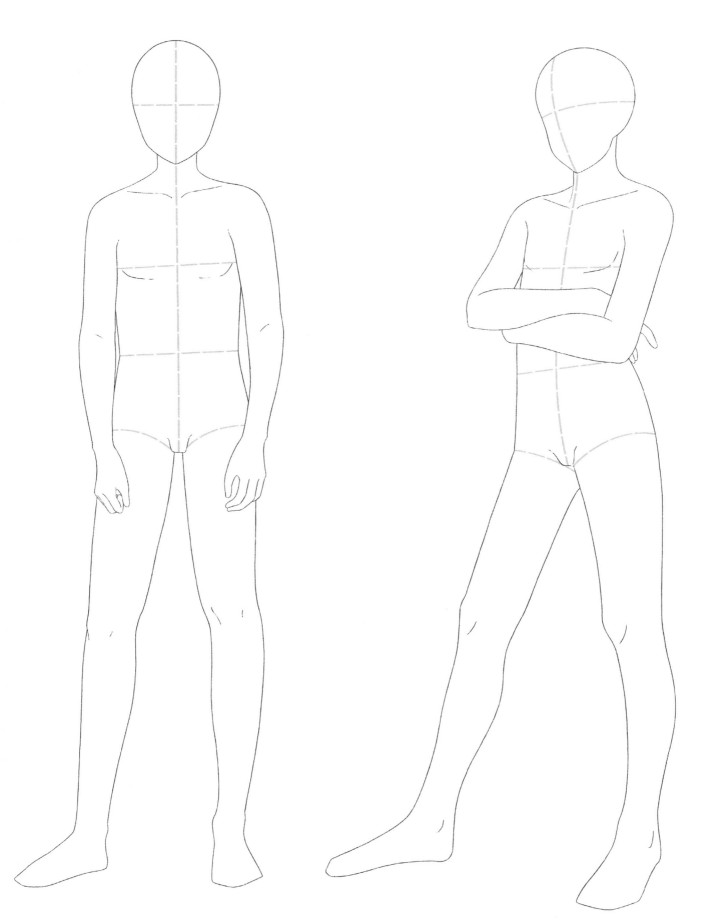

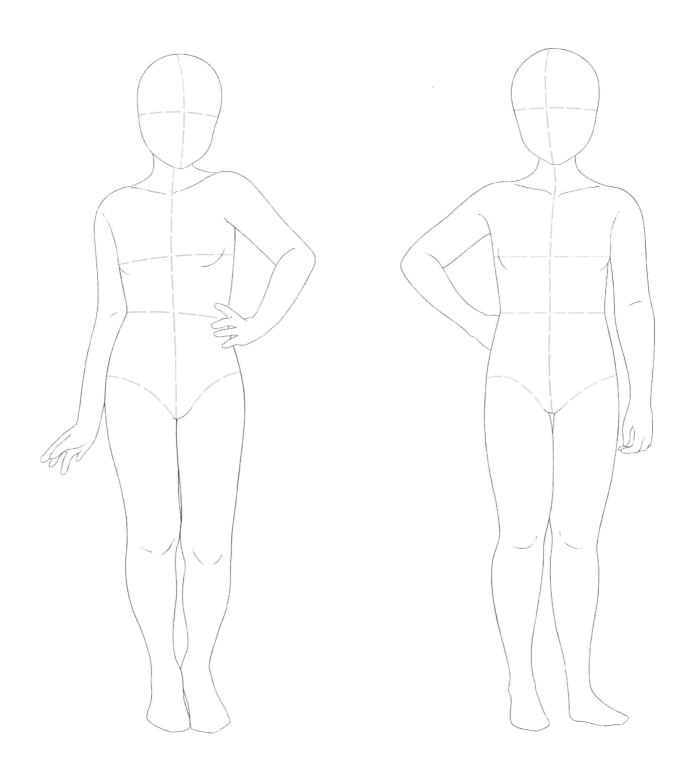

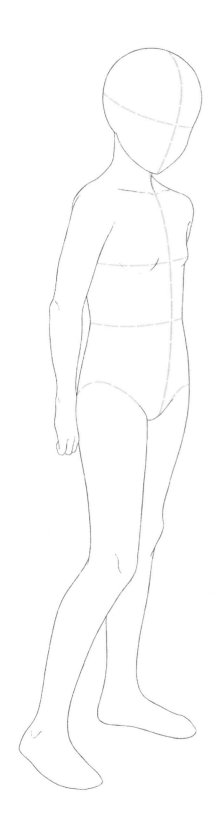
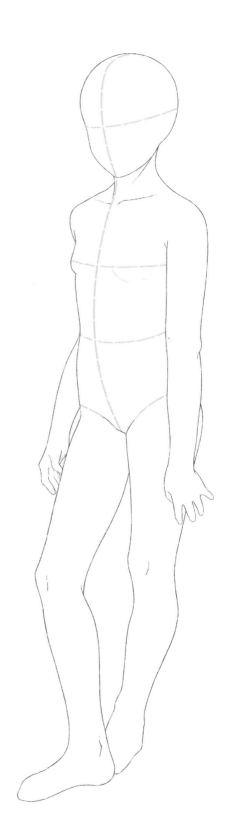

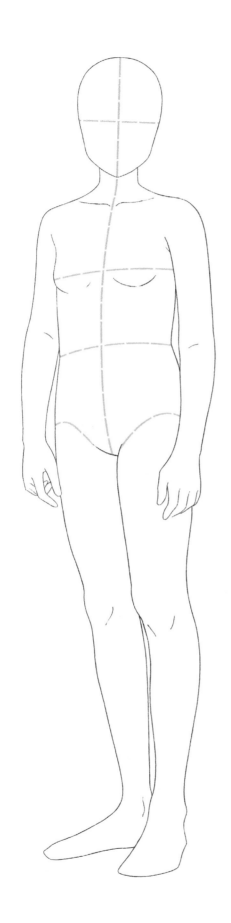
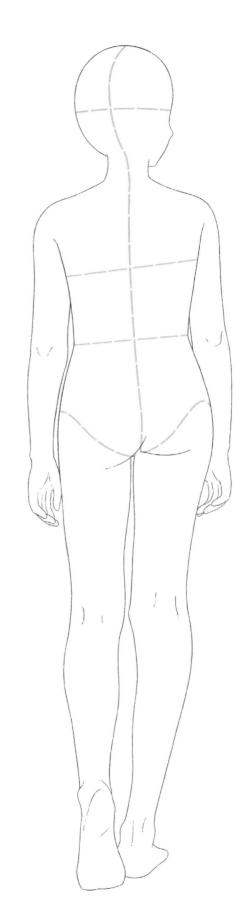

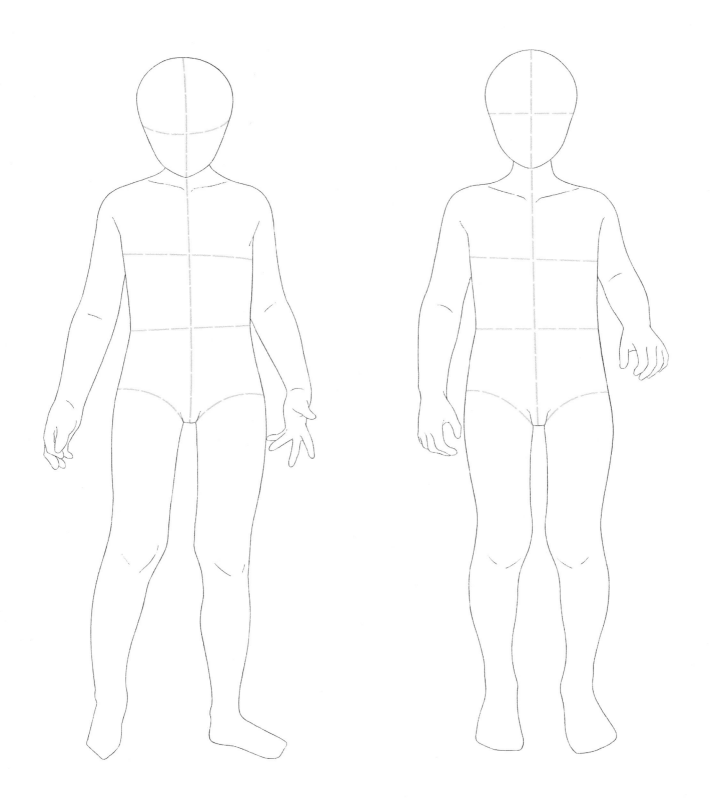

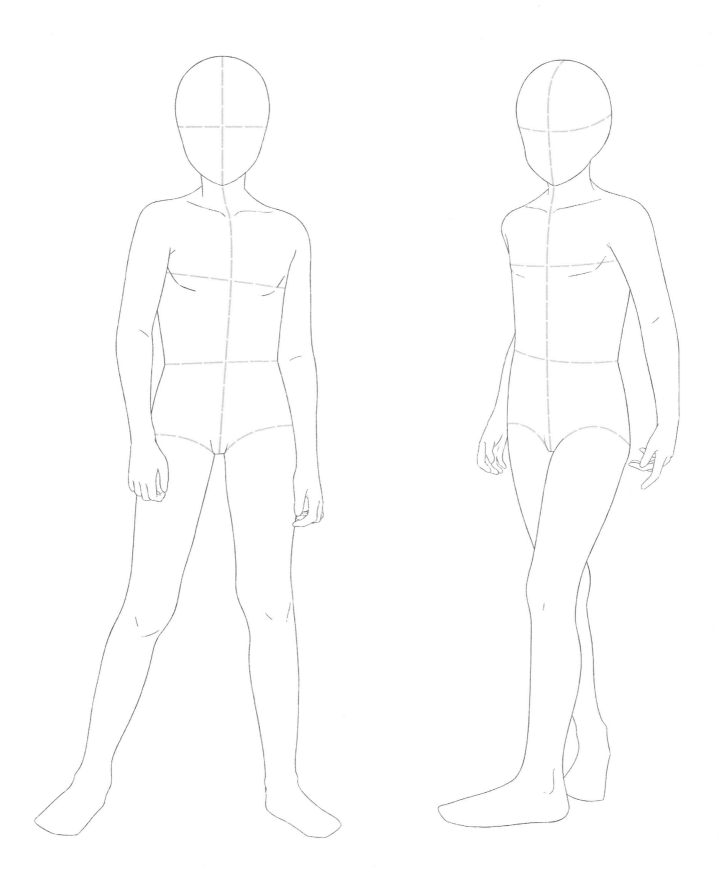

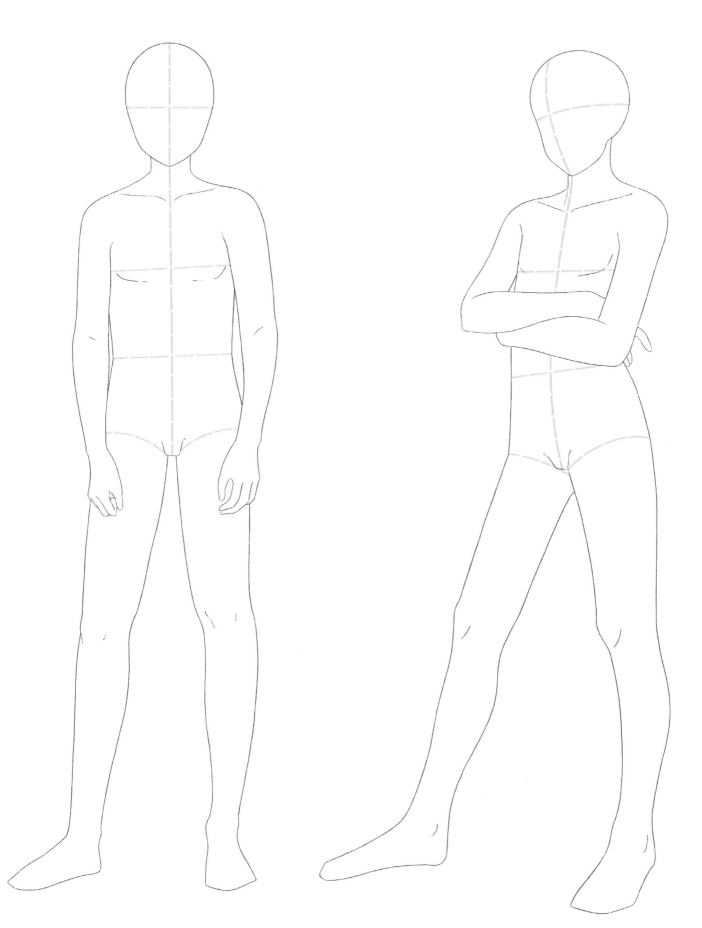

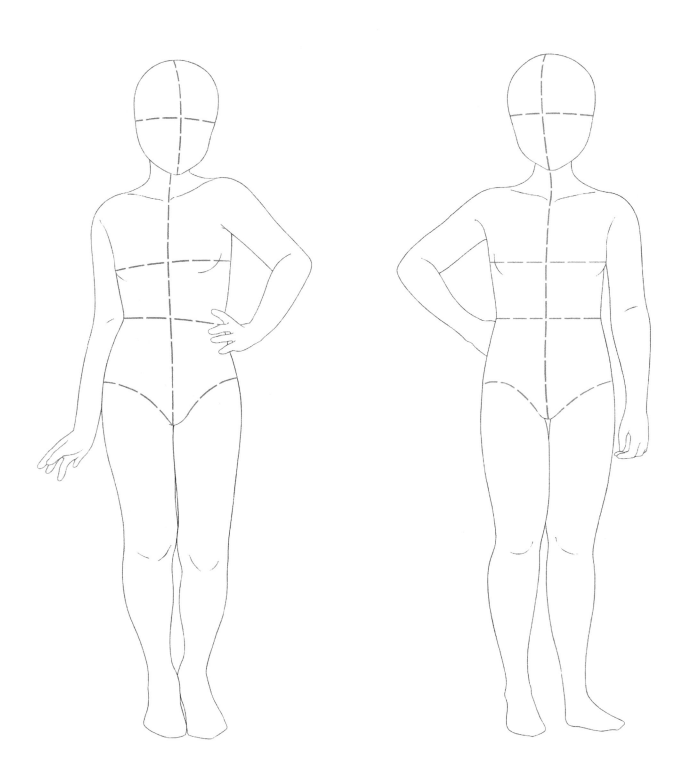

JOIN US AND GET 2 FASHION FIGURE TEMPLATES FOR FREE!

https://content.byebye.studio/designersupplynews

 @_byebye_studio_

 /byebyestudio

BYE
BYE
PAPER

Made in the USA
Las Vegas, NV
02 June 2023

72849123R00070